WHERE THE PLACE CALLED MORNING LIES

Also by Frank Graham, Jr.

DISASTER BY DEFAULT:
POLITICS AND
WATER POLLUTION

SINCE SILENT SPRING

MAN'S DOMINION:
THE STORY OF
CONSERVATION IN AMERICA

For children (with Ada Graham)

THE GREAT AMERICAN
SHOPPING CART

WILDLIFE RESCUE

PUFFIN ISLAND

THE MYSTERY OF
THE EVERGLADES

WHERE THE PLACE CALLED MORNING LIES

Frank Graham, Jr.

The Viking Press   New York

Copyright © 1966, 1970, 1973 by Frank Graham, Jr.
All rights reserved
First published in 1973 by The Viking Press, Inc.
625 Madison Avenue, New York, N.Y. 10022
Published simultaneously in Canada by
The Macmillan Company of Canada Limited
SBN 670-76123-0
Library of Congress catalog card number: 73-2650
Printed in U. S. A.

Acknowledgment is made to the following for permission to use material quoted:

Margaret Coffin Halvosa: From *Saltwater Farm* by Robert P. Tristram Coffin. Copyright 1937 by The Macmillan Company. Copyright © renewed 1965 by Margaret Coffin Halvosa.

Harcourt Brace Jovanovich, Inc.: From *Complete Poems 1913–1962* by E. E. Cummings.

The Viking Press, Inc. From *The Portable Dorothy Parker.* Copyright 1944 by Dorothy Parker. Copyright © renewed 1972 by Lillian Hellman.

—

Chapter 10 originally appeared, in somewhat different form, as an article in *American Heritage*. Portions of several other chapters originally appeared in *Audubon* and *Sports Illustrated*. The author is grateful to the editors of those publications for permission to reprint this material here.

TO ADA
who shed light and meaning
on every step of the way

✠ CONTENTS

"Where the place called morning lies!"
—EMILY DICKINSON

PROLOGUE

I AM SITTING HERE in the little cabin on the shore of Narraguagus Bay where I write, listening to the rain drum fitfully on the shingled roof and watching the yellow leaves of poplars and birches fly past on the wind. The tide is nearly high, splashing over the granite ledges below the cabin. I see my sailboat bucking at its mooring seventy-five yards offshore. Normally it is an unglamorous little craft, too blunt in its lines and too sluggish in its response to the tiller under sail, but now it has swung around to face the storm, its mast at a rakish angle. The sight should give me unmixed pleasure, but autumn is well under way here and I know I am remiss in not having dragged the boat some days ago to the safety of its winter quarters ashore. A chattering fire in the wood stove behind my chair echoes the rain's monody.

I have just finished reading *The New York Times* that arrived in this morning's mail. (Each issue is a day late, and sometimes two, when it reaches this town on the Maine coast, 505 miles northeast of Times Square.) In the latest *Times* there was a review of a new collection of Dylan Thomas's poems. The reviewer said that the poems did not give him goose pimples as they once did. He said that Thomas traded in "immediacy," and then added, "But Thomas does ask a lot with his foxes and ferns, towers and tides, herons and wrens. Push back the question as we may, it is there on the tip of our tongues: 'What has this to do with me now?' "

Apparently, the man who wrote the review feels that prison reform, women's lib, Vietnam, and busing squabbles are of more moment than tides and herons. Perhaps he is right, but I tend to believe he is not. Like Pater I want to get as many "pulsations" as possible into my given time, which means that I want to be where the action is, and after thirty-six years of living and traveling over much of the world I found the action here in a Maine fishing village. The tide rises higher on the rocks below me, and a gull sweeps past my window on motionless wings, encased in a blast of wind.

In 1961 my wife, Ada, and I moved to Maine, and three years later I began to write my first book about the "environmental crisis." The two steps were closely related. The satisfaction and excitement in living close to the natural world that had impelled me toward Maine had its counterpart in the anxiety I began to feel as this world became increasingly threatened by man's ingenuity.

Although it is often described as a "backwater" of modern America, at least one isolated section of the eastern Maine coast received national attention in recent years. Government and industry conceived a plan to build a huge oil terminal and refinery near the town of Machiasport. A summer visitor to Machiasport, approaching either by land or by sea, is likely to come upon the town damply wrapped in one of the fogs for which it is famous. Even fog cannot diminish the loveliness of that part of the coast. There is life in the fog—purposeful cormorants, stately great blue herons, the flashing white wing patches of guillemots and, if one is both fortunate and alert, a puffin straying from the colony at Machias Seal Island ten miles offshore. Through the mist's ragged hem one catches glimpses of spruce-covered islands rising from Machias Bay on granite pedestals.

But when the sun shines through, bringing out the red from the rocks and the whiteness from gulls' breasts as a clown's mask draws laughter from a child, this coast is something else again. "How can a man walk out on this peninsula and still want to bring the oil industry to Machiasport?" a Maine newspaperman asked as he stood on the rocks below the town.

The same question may be asked about any other area of the coast between Bar Harbor and Eastport, and about any other heavy industry. It is a vexing question, and one not always answered to conservationists' satisfaction by men of good will. For there is another side to this stretch of northern coast: most of it is encompassed within Washington County. This county, whose 2420 square miles are chiefly forests, lakes, and bogs, is larger than the state of Delaware but holds only 29,000 people, nearly all of them in a narrow file along the coast. Nine of its towns have less than a hundred people. There is poverty here, manifest in the sagging tarpaper shacks that serve as homes for some of the residents. Jobs are scarce and wages generally low.

To disregard this remote county's residue of misery would be both foolish and heartless. The region cries out for an infusion of viable industry to give it a stronger hold on its young (sorely tempted by more prosperous cities to the south) and to quicken the life pulse of those who choose to remain. Most industries today note its remoteness from centers of population, with the attendant difficulties of transportation, and decide to set up shop elsewhere. The sea, the forest, and the "summer people" (all depending on a healthy environment) continue to be the bedrock of the county's economy.

But heavy industries have always depended on natural resources, too. Their isolation, their remoteness from markets or transportation, do not matter once Persons of Influence, sitting at their desks hundreds or thousands of miles away, conceive a plan to use those resources. It has happened in the Amazon's steamy jungles, in the remote sands of Arabia, and on Alaska's bleak North Slope. "The potent impulse," someone has called it, "The fructifying thought!" The impulse speeds across continents and seeks out the riches to be had for the asking, blighting the land, if need be, and the lives of the people who inhabit it.

When Ada and I moved to this part of the world it seemed safe for some years to come from the exploitation and destruction visited upon most of America to the south and west. But everything in this world is connected. Technology only hastens the response at one end of the line or the other. My new home, which some called a "backwater of America," and which at any rate seemed to exist in isolation not only from the alleged benefits but also from the obvious ills of modern life, turned out on closer inspection to be vulnerable, too. Its vulnerability is a matter of degree, so that when I read about the troubles of other Americans in the cities and suburbs I may react with pity or disgust but never with complacency. We are all under siege.

It is common enough to fall in love with a place that is not one's original home, and writers are notorious for going a step further and dashing off books about this experience in the heat of their passion. So far I have happily escaped the compulsion to write a book about *Getting Away From It All to Lead the Good Life Down East.* But it occurred to me that other people might be interested in reading about a special part of America whose small population and limited industrial development make clear the sources of change that elsewhere fade into a haze of complexity.

Like everyone else, my neighbors and I are profoundly affected by what happens thousands of miles away, though even here the connection is seldom clear at first glance. This illusory detachment gives modern life its eerie quality. An agronomist reaches a conclusion in Washington, a fisheries biologist states a theory in Moscow, a marine engineer solves a problem in Tokyo, an oilman sticks a pin into a wall-size map in Houston or Los Angeles—and life is altered here in eastern Maine.

Take that Washington agronomist, for instance. He decides that potatoes may be grown better in Idaho or blueberries may be grown better in Michigan than in eastern Maine, and government funds follow his decision. Eastern Maine becomes a little more impoverished. That biologist in Moscow decides this is a good year to sweep up all the haddock in the North Atlantic, and a massive, modern fishing fleet appears off the New England coast to shoulder aside its less adaptable competitors. Eastern Maine is further impoverished. That engineer in Tokyo makes a new advance on modern industry's struggle to refine "economies of scale," and thus a bigger and better supertanker goes into production; its draft is so great that ports deep enough to accommodate it along the eastern coast of the United States can be found only in Maine. The oilman in Houston or Los Angeles locates one of those potential deep-water ports at Machiasport or Eastport, and a quiet county and its people may be overwhelmed by change before they are aware of all its consequences. A desert war, an African *coup d'état*, or a disaster at sea—and someone else sees that a Maine coastal village may play a role in the realignment of the international oil industry. Again, life here is altered. Events such as these touch all of us more rapidly and acutely today than they ever did before.

But it seems to me that the book I am writing would be simply a statistical report if it did not set the human figure in the community and in the environment on which the community depends. I think it is important for the reader to know something about the writer: what he was like before, why he came to feel the way he does, and how he tries to come to grips with the contradictions that face all of us in our lives today. So the view the reader will find here is essentially personal. This is a book about one man's road, my own, to a special place, what I found there, and why I am concerned about its future.

In that sense the story is personal. In another sense, however, it is universal because, though my priorities may not be everyone's, I am grappling with the same forces that change life for all of us.

My book is not a paean to a place or a people, because I like to carp as well as anybody else. But I hope it is a yea-statement, in the sense that E. E. Cummings's sonnet is:

> i thank you God for most this amazing
> day:for the leaping greenly spirits of trees
> and a blue true dream of sky;and for everything
> which is natural which is infinite which is yes

"Yes" is the key word here, to say *yes* to oneself and *yes* to the world around one. Some people have bad luck and their natural inclination to say *yes* becomes stifled. They come to look on the natural world as their enemy. They want to pave it over, and cage it up, and douse it with chemicals. They think that practical considerations force them to say *no.*

I don't pretend that either the man or the place I describe in this book is "typical." Yet the problems they face are much the same that other people and places face today. I hope to get across the idea that it is a practical consideration to say *yes* to the world around us. Then perhaps we can admit that even a poet, singing of tides and herons, and foxes and ferns, still has something to say to us.

PART ✠ ONE
Getting There

1

THE ROAD
DOWN EAST

I ❧ IT MUST BE SAID at the start that, judged by my origins, I am an unlikely country man. My father was born in Harlem, my mother in Brooklyn, and I in a private hospital on Manhattan's West Side, in the neighborhood where Lincoln Center stands today. But, until I was married, I had lived in the city only as a toddler. By the time I was old enough to walk our family had embarked on a somewhat nomadic existence that led us into and out of six different homes on Long Island, in Connecticut, and in New York's Westchester County.

My father was a sports columnist for the old New York *Sun* and later the *Journal-American*. On weekends, if he was not covering a game at Yankee Stadium or the Yale Bowl, he enjoyed his strolls in the woods that always grew close by whatever house we were living in at the time. For him these walks were not voyages of discovery but social occasions, to be undertaken with relatives, friends, dogs, and walking sticks, with a rye-on-the-rocks waiting at the end of the trail. He couldn't have distinguished an otter from a weasel, or a trailing arbutus from a cardinal flower. (Once he took part in a "celebrities" quiz show, and flunked out when the quizmaster asked if beavers gnawed down trees; he must have thought it was simply a quaint invention from one of Kipling's *Just So Stories*.) His only contact with "nature" came through his friendship with John Kieran, whom he roomed with for a while during the days when they covered the New York Giants for their papers. My father used to chuckle over memories of their walks through public parks, when he would whistle softly out of one side of his mouth and send the noted naturalist tiptoeing into the shrubbery in search of nonexistent birds. Newspapermen used to be great practical jokers.

And so for many years the woods and fields were for me essentially bland countenances, attractive in their expanse and sense of mystery, but lacking in distinguishing detail. I couldn't see the trees for the forest. I gratefully inhaled but did not identify the aromas of the woods, I rolled and played on the nameless flowers of the field. Boy Scouts and hiking were diversions, but filial emulation directed my passions toward baseball. Household talk about the Yankees and Giants is among my earliest memories, and a person whose name I understood to be Bay Bruth was apparently very special indeed. When, later on, Lou Gehrig gave my father one of his old first baseman's mitts to take home to me, word of my prize spread through the neighborhood. I was invited to join a local team, composed of other twelve-year-olds, called the Wykagyl Whackers. My glove and I were assigned to first base. Under the delusion that the glove, like Zeus's shield, imparted certain powers to its bearer, the manager went so far as to write my name into the cleanup slot in his batting order. One game served to relieve him of that delusion, and I was demoted to a slot more in keeping with my earnest poke-hitting.

I can think of no vital way in which I was consciously affected by the lure of the natural world until I was nearly eighteen years old, and then its action was indirect. America was already at war with Germany and Japan. I had always loved books and movies about the sea (the first book I ever read was called *Tommy Cat the Sailor*), so there was an element of romance about the Navy that I couldn't find in the newsreel pictures of soldiers and marines slogging through alien mud. Perhaps that was what drew me into a Navy recruiting office shortly before I would have become eligible for the draft. But beyond romance there were other fascinations in the sea, vague yet real. I think that the rhythm of the sea's movement is a part of us all. Roger Kahn once remarked to Robert Frost about how children respond naturally to the rhythms in poetry. "Yes," Frost said, "because their hearts beat, and they see the waves." The moving seas touch a primitive chord in our own pulse, too.

And nothingness. There is the lure of nothingness in the sea. The scientist, who is aware of the sea's teeming life and the component elements of sea water itself (which he can distinguish by chemical analysis from spindrift, the sea's airy chaff), has left this notion forever behind him. The hypnotic nothingness of the sea, like the nonutilitarian purity of bird song, is part of his lost innocence. Utterly naïve (ignorant and unobservant, some would insist, and it may be only another way of putting it), I spent two years aboard an escort carrier in the Pacific and took part in several of the great sea battles of the war. But what I remember best was the sea's blank face on long cloudless days and the phosphorescent fire that whirled away in the ship's wake during my night watch on the fantail. Intimations of mortality overwhelmed me. Yet the sea, replacing hellfire with an acceptance of oblivion, took away the terror of death that my childhood religion had kindled.

I never recovered from the sea, as so many other men and women never recovered from the war. The postwar years were busy and secure, but tainted with the futility which we see now was a mark of the times. I commuted from the suburbs to Columbia University in Manhattan. During vacations I worked at the New York *Sun*. In my spare time I drank beer,

sat in stadiums watching other men play games, and indis-
criminately haunted disreputable dance halls and tea dances
at fashionable girls' schools. Since a high percentage of my
friends attended Catholic colleges, I spent a high percentage of
my spare time arguing religion. I listened respectfully to most
of the arguments for a just and personal God, but there was
one difficulty I was never able to overcome. Perhaps if I had
been more of a Darwinian at the time and had seen the
dividing line between species, including man, less distinctly I
would not have felt so strongly about the problem of animal
suffering. It was Adam and Eve who sinned and fell from
grace. If there is a just God, why should the other animals,
given neither a blemished soul nor a stake in heaven, suffer the
most unspeakable pain here in this world?

In any case, I had entered what Louis Halle calls "the
hive." My world was made up of buildings, cars, commuter
trains, stadiums, and (all too seldom) lovers' lanes, and I went
my self-important way as unconscious as the drone that this
artificial world depended for its existence on certain processes
in the greater natural world outside. I am not suggesting that
my life in those years was a nightmare. It was, in fact, very
pleasurable and probably worked some of the silliness out of
me. New York City with its social variety and stimulation
seems to me an indispensable part of one's education at a
certain period in life. And there were a good many laughs
along the way.

Most of the laughs occurred when I entered a hive within
the hive, when I disappeared down that alluring rabbit hole
into the perpetual daydream-world of professional baseball.
The New York *Sun* had collapsed a few months before I was to
graduate from Columbia and join its staff. With the available
jobs on the city's newspapers further depleted (I never would
have thought of leaving New York for a job in a smaller city),
I finally found a job in the public-relations department of the
Brooklyn Dodgers.

It may have been a shortcoming in me, or so many of my

colleagues there said, but I rather liked the team's owner, Walter O'Malley. I thought that very often he wanted to do the right thing, but he had an infallible instinct for phrasing matters in the worst possible way. During a well-attended meeting to discuss the team's postseason trip to Japan, O'Malley emphatically turned down a proposal to bring along an elderly member of the board of directors.

"The trip's likely to kill him," O'Malley commented dispassionately. "What would we do with a *body* on our hands in Japan?"

It was hard to dislike such frankness. Moreover, O'Malley was a businessman by training and disposition, and he didn't really know very much about baseball. He spoke of a ballplayer's skill with the forced heartiness of a homosexual praising pretty girls. Jackie Robinson, our star player then, disliked and distrusted him. Robinson used to call me during the winter months to find out what O'Malley was saying about him.

The airtight world of professional baseball took on enormous dimensions for its inmates. We lived not by the Constitution of the United States but by the "Rule Book," the "Blue Book," and the Commissioner's edicts. We usually worked seven days a week during the spring and summer, spending weekdays at the office and nights and weekends at the ball park. I was living in the city then, and the only trees I saw were those on the other side of the fence in Prospect Park as I walked past on my way from the subway station to Ebbets Field. The only birds I saw were pigeons that roosted on the grandstand rafters and enraged the "Flatbush Faithful" with their droppings. Spring meant spring training, or our special world's rebirth, if you will. Rain implied not a blooming earth but somebody's three-runs-batted-in washed out by a curtailed game. I can think of no more dismal sight than a ball park on a sodden night, the crowd huddled glumly under umbrellas, watching the sterile rain pound into the glistening tarpaulins that have been rolled out to cover the infield.

II ❧   BY THE MIDDLE 1950s my own life had changed and opened up. I had married. On our first date, most of which we spent cooped up at a party in a stuffy Manhattan apartment, Ada wanted to walk off the stuffiness. A wild storm battered the city that night, and for an hour or more we walked the streets in the pour of wind and rain that came off the Hudson River, soaked through yet intensely excited. I suppose I was already in love, and I responded to the storm that night, too. For the first time since those long dreamy days on the Pacific I knew there was a life outside the hive as real as anything in it.

Ada had grown up in a more utilitarian relationship with the natural world than I had. Her father had tried to squeeze a Depression living out of a small farm in southern Ohio, delaying the inevitable migration into a Dayton industrial plant. This was not the "back to the land" idyll that college boys and girls dream about today. It was monotonous work and very little fun, and the children shared their parents' daily grind. It would have been a luxury to gaze sentimentally at animals or to idealize "nature" from that perspective. The soybeans failed or were a glut on the market. Squirrel meat, sometimes provided by a sharpshooting uncle, was a welcome addition to the table. Chicken was not a meal that came wrapped in plastic. The family chickens sickened and sometimes died, while cleaning and plucking the harvested birds was not a mechanized process but a dirty and laborious family chore. Games and movies and anecdotes of New York professional life had not been a part of Ada's childhood, as they had been of mine.

But from her earliest memories she had been a voracious reader. She haunted the local public library as most kids haunt the local Dairy Joy, and she was soon aware of various worlds beyond southern Ohio's rolling hills. After college she came to New York, where she worked for a while at the New York Society Library. Ada was never wholly sold on the city, as are so many young people who flee from small Midwestern towns. Still, there was no sentimentality about an idealized rural background. The family farm was abandoned, and it was Dayton's heavy industry that gave her parents at last a few of the luxuries of life they had been breaking their backs to try to earn on the farm. The countryside that Ada had known as a child disappeared under industrial parks and shopping centers and the competitively immaculate lawns of suburbia. A certain hardness had gone out of life there, but in the process it was losing touch with its wellsprings. Blandness may be preferable to hardship, but is there another alternative? (In recent years even her parents' pleasant suburban home fell victim to sprawl; builders bought the open land on the other side of the tree-shaded stream that flowed leisurely behind their home, cut down all the lovely old trees, and dubbed their new development "Shady Brook Acres.")

I think that most of us feel an awful loneliness and restlessness when we are cut off from our wild wellsprings. This feeling is not a renunciation of civilization but an affirmation of our oneness with life itself. "What would the world be," asked that sophisticated Jesuit, Gerard Manley Hopkins, "once bereft of wet and of wildness?" I wondered, too, that first evening with Ada, and I was charmed by a librarian who didn't mind getting her feet wet.

I left my job with the Dodgers soon after Ada and I were married. Not even Columbia's literature courses had completely dampened my early desire to write, and now I went to work as a writer and editor for *Sport* magazine. One of the ancillary benefits (as the sports promoters used to say) of my new job was that, for the first time since junior high school, I was presented with a genuine summer vacation. Ada and I rented a friend's cottage at Fire Island, where I planned to renew my acquaintance with the sea. We took with us a collection of paperback guides to the shore animals, wild flowers, and birds and, though people do not ordinarily go to Fire Island to observe exactly those forms of life, we were prepared to look and learn. On long walks along the beach we sorted out and identified the plants and shells we discovered. We poked around in the debris hurled up by the breakers. I came to look upon the sea with new interest for what it revealed in the variety of matter, living and dead, that it sloughed off.

But the birds were the true revelation. I had read about many kinds of birds, but most of their names I associated with distant lands or impenetrable jungles. Only the gulls, English sparrows, starlings, robins, and pigeons had seemed real to me; the others had remained as remote as basilisks. Now, as I looked closely, I noticed distinctions. The bird that was rusty underneath was not a robin at all. The reddish color, I saw, did not cover the breast, and when the bird flew off at my cautious approach it revealed flashing white tail feathers. I had identified my first towhee! For the first time I truly watched a swallow sweep low over the beach and saw the glory of its flight. With its wings held back like fins, the swallow hung momentarily over a damp place in the dunes, then darted off like a frightened fish. In full sweep it made flying look almost *too* easy; it seemed to be flying under wraps, like a man racing a little boy across the lawn.

In walking along the beach or through the sandy wastes down the center of the island I found that the joy in identifying birds came not so much from an ever-lengthening list of "conquests," but rather from the interplay between observation and labeling. To detect the characteristics that made a bird distinct was to be able to put a label on it, and when I came upon the bird again I would be able to fill in the secondary details I had originally missed. Through this echoic pattern the infinite diversity of nature began to take on new meaning for me. When we returned from the shore we looked at New York from a different perspective. The fortress city, traditionally a refuge from the real or imagined menace of the countryside, was still vulnerable to nature. Vestiges of the natural world managed to slip through the gates. We needed only to open our eyes to see them.

At the private school where Ada taught on the West Side there was that rare species of his day, a science teacher who was familiar with wild things. We trailed Bob Mathews around the city and learned where to look for birds. We went with him to city parks, large and small. We learned to distinguish our native white-throated and song sparrows from the despised English sparrow. We noticed herons flying over the city, a sight that boggled the mind.

Mathews invited us to take part in the National Audubon Society's annual Christmas Bird Count. He was to cover a strip on Manhattan's East Side from 125th Street to the Battery. At dawn on the appointed morning, carrying binoculars and a Roger Tory Peterson guidebook and wearing our warmest and most unfashionable clothes, we met Mathews in front of an automat on Fourteenth Street. No one was about except derelicts and bird watchers, and before setting out we ate a warm bowl of oatmeal in the company of both. A tip on the local birders' grapevine sent us to Bryant Park to locate a slate-colored junco, but we had to settle for pigeons and sparrows. We walked across the East River on a bridge to Welfare Island and counted more rats than birds. And we ended that frigid day by watching gulls inspect the streets for scraps near the Fulton Fish Market.

But watching birds is not an end in itself. Birds, like flowers and otters and butterflies, are endlessly diverting and indispensable companions on our journey into eternity. So are apes and aardvarks and alligators. ("What's a reptile ever done for *me*?" asks the practical man. Well, comes the retort, one of the evolving reptile's contributions to his fellow creatures was the penis.) The important thing here is that when a man reaches out to another free species he has broken out of the isolation increasingly imposed on him by industrial civilization. He has reached across the barrier of polyester fibers, processed potatoes, and conditioned air to touch something that endures. He has restored palpability to his world.

We left New York for Europe in the spring of 1959. I had become a free-lance writer and, with the city going sour, there seemed no reason to stay. "You're fleeing from reality," a friend scolded, and we had to laugh. Reality in New York had become synonymous with "life in the raw," with degradation. One could still find pockets of reality there. Parks provided a semblance of the fresh world outside, though the engineers were dissecting them into progressively smaller segments by networks of highways. Italian markets on Bleecker Street or Ninth Avenue still offered for sale fruits and vegetables that stirred the senses and did not look as if they had been fashioned by trolls from directions taken down over the telephone. Snow could still bring the city to a stop. But life within the hive had become, finally, artificial and airless. Along ever-grimier streets the sickly trees dropped their catkins on the pavement in a kind of botanical onanism.

We sailed on a Dutch freighter from Hoboken to Antwerp in order to savor the approach; it would have been too jarring to encapsulate our first trip to Europe in a jet ride of a few hours. We had made no plans, we wanted only to open ourselves to the experience before us. After the first few culture-crowded weeks, we found ourselves eager to escape the big cities. Rome, London, Vienna—even magical Paris—were too close to what we had just abandoned, and so our years in Europe consisted chiefly of prolonged residence in the vicinity of three smaller cities, with occasional forays into the tourist centers.

We lived for a time in Fiesole, a village in the hills overlooking Florence. As we left and drove into the Alps, leaving the olive trees and *pasta* behind us, I realized for the first time how much I missed the northern landscape and northern cooking. We settled in Innsbruck, among evergreens and Wiener schnitzel. Through the windows of the rooms we rented from Frau Obexer in an old building on Mariatheresienstrasse we looked on the enormous façade of the *Nordkette* that brooded over the city. And in the end we found ourselves back in the sun, occupying an ancient farmhouse and twenty acres outside Arles in Provence. In the late afternoons we drove into the Camargue to watch the great flights of flamingos strung out darkly against the setting sun. A friend wrote from New York: "Why is it that you always choose the Philadelphias of this world to live in?"

For more than two years we lived inexpensively, and sometimes almost primitively, in Europe, close to the outdoors and with a sense of being alive that we had never felt in the city. During a Tuscan drought we rose at dawn to collect water for the day in old wine bottles. During the brief Provençal winter we warmed ourselves by burning olive wood in a huge fireplace. We lived without ice cubes and hot running water and central heat—little things, perhaps, but a reminder that even the necessities of life don't always come through wires and pipes or wrapped up in plastic.

But there was something deeper than the trivial game of "roughing it." (Americans will never really know again, even in our poorest or most remote areas, what "roughing it" was really like for our ancestors; if a person has the strength or the will to call for help today, whether he is lost in a jungle or starving in a ghetto, a helicopter or a social worker is at hand to bail him out.) What touched us most deeply, I think, was the integrity of the landscapes. We, like our neighbors, lived there in a real world that reflected the lives of the men and their fellow creatures who had inhabited these regions for countless years before we came. There was a sense of *place*—the landscape, whether it was Tuscan or Provençal or Tyrolean, provided a setting into which we could fit our lives sensually. That, I understand, is changing now, as so much is changing in our time, and there may come a day very soon when those landscapes and the people in them will be interchangeable. They will eat the same processed foods, wear the same synthetic fabrics, and live in the same modular houses. Then we can, with equal profit to our souls and senses, visit Dearborn or Avignon, Akron or Siena.

It was in Arles that our future was pointed out to us. Our money was running out (I was one of the few modern free-lance writers not clever enough to earn a living in Europe) and our return to America was imminent. With summer coming on, we dreaded going back to live in New York. An American couple who lived nearby suggested the Maine coast, where they had often spent their summers.

Why not? we asked ourselves. Often when we had been able to leave New York for an extended period we had driven into northern New England and found it agreeable. It was the inland regions we liked, however, for our experience with coastal towns had prejudiced us against them: they either reeked of honky-tonk or breathed quaintness through all their pores.

But our friends urged us into correspondence, and before we left Europe we had a classified ad running in the Rockland *Courier-Gazette*: "Writer, wife desire secluded, inexpensive lodgings." We came back by freighter from Marseilles (this time to delay our reabsorption into the New World) and found answers to the ad awaiting us. We chose the most likely one, then followed directions which brought us to a meeting place one afternoon in early summer on the main street of a fishing town in eastern Maine. Fog hung over the houses and dripping trees.

"I told my wife this was you coming," said Ben Harding, our prospective landlord. "I could tell by the car."

After shaking hands with the Hardings, I got back into the Dauphine we had brought home with us on the freighter and followed them out of town. We turned onto a dirt road, driving slowly because of the ruts and the thick fog. The spruce trees along the road were draped with the stringy gray lichen called old-man's-beard. The landscape was ghostly, the drive seemed endless. At last we reached a small cove, with half a dozen "camps" clustered around it. The Hardings pulled up beside the camp they wanted to rent to us and we got out and stood there, looking into the fog.

It had receded somewhat, baring an indeterminate stretch of mud flat. There was no water in sight, but the Hardings assured us it was out there someplace in the fog. The stillness was profound. No leaf rustled, no bird cried. We stared at this shrouded seascape, as if it held some exalting and momentous revelation. But for the moment it made us no overture. The sea was not ready to grant these newcomers its blessing.

The camp's chief virtue seemed to be simplicity. It had been put together from two prewar overnight cabins, so that without its honest sloping roof it would have been condemned to a trailer's crackerbox outlines. Not a building to fall in love with, hardly even a building to call home. We chatted with the Hardings, still expectant, as it were, still reluctant to commit ourselves. And then the sea forced our commitment. As we talked in front of the camp a breeze came up, stirring and tearing the fog, and the water came into view a long way out across the mud. It was simply a glint at first, like a puddle creeping under a door. Then it gained substance. Ada and I became aware of some impending event outside our previous experience. The breeze was out of the south and it seemed to push the water ahead of it up the cove, amplifying the sense of primal movement with a low soughing that sounded like a thousand people whispering "chrysalises."

Its sudden appearance out of the fog, its surface agitated by the wind, gave the water an extraordinary illusion of velocity. That it was two hours or more before the tide finally pushed its foaming front edge up the narrow sand beach in front of the camp did not alter that impression. Only a few years before I had found the sea, like the rest of the world outside my hive, a passive presence—a retreat from the menace of affairs and affronts and responsibilities in which I lived. Even when it raged in howling gales, I had found it a symbol of oblivion. The natural world, I had since come to know, was a place of endless and various experience. To dwell in its active presence was to nourish one's own sense of being alive. On that day the sea also showed me its true character. This was the rhythm I had felt in the Pacific, defined here by its inexorable advance across the mud flats, making manifest the force of sun and moon and the earth's endless spinning on this little patch of the planet. It was a recurring drama I would find hard to turn my back on.

2
WASHINGTON
COUNTY

I 𝒳   I WAS NOT THE FIRST member of my family to venture this far Down East. Some years before a couple vaguely related to me had rented a house for the summer in a small Washington County coastal town. I had known Tom and Lu all my life. They taught and lived in New York. When summer came around, they always left the city for some pleasant place in the country, in Connecticut or the Hudson River Valley or Bucks County, Pennsylvania. Both of them loved the country and were at home in it, at least for a few months. But eastern Maine was too much for them. They lasted only a week, then packed their bags and fled back to their apartment in the city.

"It was too *stark*," Lu told me later. "We were very uncomfortable."

That they had entered an unfamiliar world was not simply a fleeting emotional response on their part but a scientific fact. Years ago biologists divided North America into three major regions, Tropical, Austral, and Boreal (the latter two regions subdivided into three zones), based on the type of life they support. Central America, parts of Mexico, and the southern tip of Florida were classed as Tropical; most of the contiguous forty-eight United States as Austral; and Alaska, Canada, and the most northerly or mountainous portions of the forty-eight states as Boreal. The dividing line between the Austral and Boreal regions bisects the Maine coast at a point a little below Bar Harbor and Mount Desert Island. And so when my relatives, who were at home in the "picturesque" hardwood forests and rolling hills that nineteenth-century landscape painters had engraved on the American mind, ventured Down East they found country not only unfamiliar but actually hostile. Wind, cold, poor soils, and an inconstant sun have done their work. The hardwoods, where they survive, seem puny. The great oaks and sugar maples peter out into groves of slender birches, poplars, and red maples; the beeches have nearly reached the limit of their range so that maturing specimens invariably fall easy victim to a scale insect and disease. Tom and Lu had reached the limit of their range, too. Even the promotional slogans that extolled "the Pine Tree State" and "the rockbound coast" let them down.

Maine's majestic white pines, like the topless towers of Ilium, are a romantic memory. Back in colonial days they were in great demand as masts for the ships of His Majesty's Navy. The king's agents searched the forests for the largest specimens, then marked them with the "broad arrow" that reserved them against use for more prosaic purposes. After the Revolution, the pines were consumed by home-grown industries or used in the building of houses by the local residents. In any case, the pines never grew in enormous single stands, but in smaller clusters interspersed among other evergreens. So pines, which take eighty or ninety years to grow to maturity, have been cut and replaced along most parts of the coast by spruces, which reseed themselves more quickly.

Nor does the Maine coast present a uniformly rocky face to the sea. It is a drowned coastline, the land having been pushed down and compressed by the enormous glaciers that once covered it. As the glaciers receded and the melting ice mingled with the salt sea, the waters rose and left only the higher points of land along the coast standing dry above it. Land that had been valleys before the glacier was now flooded and turned into long narrow bays. Farther out the hilltops remained above the water's surface to compose Maine's galaxy of offshore islands. Today, though most of the remaining mainland stands above the tides on its rocky base, here and there in protected bays the rivers have accumulated thick mats of salt marshes at their mouths. Here the rivers wind through the last part of their journey to the sea, and twice a day the sea sweeps in over the marshes, bringing with it the nutrients that convert these wetlands into nurseries for marine populations. Many fish and shellfish find food and shelter in these marshes during the vulnerable early stages of life.

But an area's fascination lies in the eye of the beholder. A visitor may be enchanted by the play of breaking surf and flickering light on Maine's rugged rocks yet miss entirely the richness of life that comes together in a healthy salt marsh— plants, birds of many kinds, perhaps a hunting mammal, and, in the pools, a variety of marine creatures. Tom and Lu, settled in a protected bay where marshland and wind-whipped spruces filled the view, detected only starkness and promptly fled.

Nevertheless, it is this region's natural attributes that have drawn people here, for good or ill, throughout written history. In the late 1960s it was the deep-water harbors that attracted the oil industry. The site originally selected by the industry was Machiasport, a fishing village of 980 souls on a wooded peninsula just below Machias, the Washington County seat. A little later alternate sites for a terminal around Eastport were mentioned (sometimes by environmentalists and lobster fishermen, grasping at any diversion that would muddle the issue at Machiasport). Later still, the oilmen made their rush at Eastport.

Both localities had been removed from the limelight for a long time. During the first excitement over the oil announcement, newsmen from all the major American media flooded Machias. To lend their dispatches a jot of local color, the visiting correspondents invariably mentioned the gossip about oil development that made the rounds of Helen's, the town's most presentable eatery. Soon spot advertisements on the Machias radio station took advantage of the publicity, urging listeners to dine regularly at "world-famous Helen's." Machias, in truth, had not known such fame since the dawn of the nation's history, when its citizens fought and won the first naval battle of the Revolutionary War.

Explorers, traders, and fishermen knew eastern Maine in the sixteenth century, but it was two hundred years or more before permanent settlements sprang up there. The salt hay that grew in the marshes along the Machias River first interested the colonists, who were searching for fodder for their domestic animals. But it was the falls in the river (Machias is a corruption of the Indian "Mechises," or bad little falls) and the abundant timber upcountry that brought them to stay, as they did other colonists to all the other "millstreams" in eastern Maine. Machias was settled in 1763.

Maine was still a part of the State of Massachusetts when the Revolution broke out. During the early days of the war the British schooner *Margaretta*, under the command of a Midshipmen Moor, anchored in the Machias River. When Moor went ashore with the other officers, a resident of East Machias named Benjamin Foster was plotting an unpleasant surprise for them. Foster and his friends hoped to seize the officers, then row out and capture the warship. The plan went amiss when the British officers returned to their vessel ahead of schedule.

But Foster was undaunted. He got in touch with Jeremiah O'Brien of Machias, and the two colonists agreed on a coordinated attack. Commandeering two small vessels, they sailed down the river with their followers, armed only with muskets and pitchforks. As they approached the warship, the

British opened fire, killing two men and wounding several others. But the colonists sailed on. They closed with the warship and boarded her. In the brisk battle at close quarters that followed, the boarding party killed Midshipman Moor and captured the vessel. Then the colonists sailed their prize back up the river to Machias in triumph.

Now that the citizens of Machias had struck a blow for liberty and come away comparatively unscathed, they could scarcely be expected to sit out the rest of the war. They formed a "Plantation Committee of Safety." The new committee fitted out a local sloop with the captured guns and swivels, rechristened her *Liberty*, and sent her out into the Bay of Fundy under the command of Jeremiah O'Brien to round up more prizes. The *Liberty*'s hunt proved unsuccessful. On the return voyage to Machias, however, O'Brien learned that the British schooner *Diligent* lay at anchor off Bucks Harbor, not far from the site that the oilmen would pick for their proposed terminal and refinery nearly two hundred years later. O'Brien and Foster once more joined forces and captured the *Diligent* in a bloodless battle. The two heroes proceeded to Falmouth (now Portland) with their prisoners, and then on to Cambridge, where the Provincial Congress received them and extended the public's thanks for their "courage and good conduct."

II 🌿 EASTPORT, at the extreme eastern end of the Maine coast, came to public notice in a different sort of way. "Sixty years since," a local historian named Lorenzo Sabine wrote in 1872, "Eastport was one of the most noted places in the country. But its fame was of a kind which no people should desire; for the general impression was that its inhabitants were bold and reckless men, and earned their support by sheltering, and sharing the gains of, adventurers, smugglers and gamblers."

Like a grand courtesan, Eastport might have traced the root of its shame to its abundant natural endowments. After the Revolutionary War, fishermen from Lynn, Marblehead, Cape Ann, and other ports near Boston founded Eastport on Moose Island in Passamaquoddy Bay. They chose the site not for its natural beauty, which is considerable but because it was a convenient place to dry their fish. Great tides sweep twice a day through the barrier of islands into Passamaquoddy Bay from the Bay of Fundy (Fundy itself is descriptive, being a corruption of "Bahia Profundo," or deep bay, which it was called by Spanish explorers who visited the region). Moose Island is four and a half miles long and about a mile and a quarter wide at its thickest point. It is bounded on the south and west by the mainland United States, and on the north and east by Deer Island, Indian Island, and Campobello, all parts of Canada. Local sovereignty was not always so clear, but the fishermen of long ago did not care; they saw Moose Island and the town as only a temporary settlement.

The Revolutionary War did not clear up the question of the boundary between the new nation and Canada. Both sides agreed that the boundary was determined by the St. Croix River, but they could not agree on which of the three rivers in that area was the one called St. Croix by early French explorers. (The one in the middle proved to be the real St. Croix at last, but for a long time the United States and Great Britain each pointed to the river boundary which would mean the largest slice of territory for itself.) People referred to the region as "on the lines."

Eastport came into its own in 1807 as serious trouble broke out between the two countries. Congress laid an embargo on all international trade to and from American ports. As Eastport lay within sight of British territory, smugglers understandably presumed that it would make an ideal way station between Canada and the United States. Early in the summer of 1808 more than a dozen ships rode at anchor in Eastport's harbor, their holds packed with flour and other articles in demand for the illicit trade. In one week 30,000 barrels of flour—probably 160,000 barrels during the year—were landed at Eastport, destined for the Canadian ports nearby. There were no large warehouses available, of course. The flour and other goods were piled on the beaches, just above the tide's reach.

A collector of customs and armed guards were stationed by the United States Government at Eastport in an attempt to stem the traffic. Gunboats lurked offshore. Yet the flour, which was worth only five dollars a barrel in the United States but twelve dollars a barrel if smuggled into Canada, continued to disappear from the stocks on the beaches. "It is certain that corruption was not unknown, and individuals were false to their trust," a local historian has said. Sentinels, posted to see that the goods did not leave until bound for another United States port, were paid fifty cents for each barrel spirited away under their inattentive gaze. Even Indian canoes were pressed into service to ferry goods to Campobello and other Canadian ports across Passamaquoddy Bay. Shots were fired at the fleeing boats by honest sentinels and sailors. British cutters stood ready to defend the smugglers' crafts once they had reached Canadian waters.

The traffic was not wholly one-sided. Gypsum was smuggled into the United States in large quantities and at little risk. The American merchant who received the shipment invariably informed on himself. The collector of customs would promptly seize the shipment and, following ordinary procedure, put it up for auction. A Maine historian has described the result: "At the sale, opposing bidders—where all were alternately alike situated and did the same thing—were of course few; and the owner purchased it much at his own price, besides receiving, on settlement with the collector, his share of the proceeds as the informer."

As war approached between the two nations, acrimony

flourished except "on the lines," where Eastporters coexisted peacefully with their Canadian neighbors and fellow smugglers. This blissful condition lasted almost until the end of the War of 1812, when Great Britain decided to settle the boundary dispute in its own favor. The only obstacle to Moose Island's capture was the battery blockhouse, named Fort Sullivan, that the United States Government had erected there in 1810. A full-color booklet prepared recently by the Washington County Board of Commissioners to celebrate the region's past and present glories describes the action:

Fort Sullivan's big moment came on July 11, 1814, when a British fleet of a dozen warships of two hundred guns with troop transports hove into sight. Fort Sullivan with its six officers, 80 men and nine guns surrendered upon demand. Though there was no defense attempted against the odds, there was the satisfaction of knowing that England had sent its best against them, for the British fleet was under the command of Sir Thomas Hardy, who commanded the *Victory* at Trafalgar, taking over when Lord Nelson was mortally wounded. Sir Thomas made the Buckman House his residence.

Eastport residents suffered few real hardships under the occupation; the British considered them subjects of the Crown and not a conquered population. It was not until 1818 that a special commission determined the identity of the St. Croix. The British thereupon returned Eastport to the United States just in time for it to accompany the rest of Maine into separate statehood in 1820. Eastport's leading citizens presented the departing British commander with a letter, telling him how much they appreciated the "magnanimity and uprightness" of the occupying force.

During the rest of the nineteenth century Eastport shared the comparative prosperity that the sea provided for eastern Maine. Sardine canning became an important source of income. Eastport even entertained hopes that it would grow into an important railroad and tourist center. But the prosperity of eastern Maine declined with its fleet of sailing ships. Ships no longer set out from Maine ports on voyages to distant lands; the coastal trade declined. This part of the coast lapsed into isolation, far from the routes of modern trade. As Henry Beston pointed out, the last survivors of the era were not the fearless old ship captains but the parrots they had brought back from fabled ports and who outlived them by many years.

Eastport later lived through one moment of illusory grandeur. If Passamaquoddy Bay had not brought the town riches in trade or tourism, its enormous tides still might become the source of gold and glory. After World War I an engineer named Dexter Cooper conceived the idea of harnessing those tides to create electric power. His plan was relatively simple. The bay's islands form a nearly continuous barrier between it and the Bay of Fundy. Cooper planned to build a series of dams that would close off the gaps in this barrier. On high tide water would be permitted to flow into Passamaquoddy Bay, which he designated the "receiving pool." As the tide ebbed the gates into Passamaquoddy Bay would be closed and those between it and the adjoining "discharging pool" of Cobscook Bay would be opened. On its way into Cobscook Bay the water would turn the turbines of the huge power plant proposed for Eastport, thus creating electricity, and then flow back into the Bay of Fundy.

The scheme promised many advantages. Drought and flood, two of the drawbacks of river hydroelectric projects, would be eliminated. There are few occurrences, natural or artificial, on which man can depend, but orderly procession of the tides is one of them. The flow of water would be powerful and constant (with allowances for spring and neap tides), as enduring as the moon itself. Besides, no farms and villages would need to be flooded to create a reservoir for the project, an enormous source of power would be made available to the Northeast, and a depressed region would gain a needed lift.

The project was expensive but, from an engineer's standpoint, feasible.

Dexter soon won over a valuable ally. Campobello, in Passamaquoddy Bay, happened to number among its "rusticators," or summer residents, the young Franklin Delano Roosevelt. Roosevelt had often sailed in the bay, growing familiar with its islands and tides. He was impressed by Cooper's plan.

Not much came of the project during the 1920s. The private utility companies viewed it as a threat, and so did their friends and spokesmen in the highest offices of the federal government. But when Roosevelt became President in 1933 he added "Quoddy" to the public power projects (including TVA) that he enthusiastically supported. Canada, too, was interested, and a vast international project seemed about to come into being. "Quoddy Village" sprang up alongside Eastport on Moose Island to house the army of workers who would build the dams and the power plant. Eastport became a boom town. The people of Maine stirred with the excitement that comes of an association with mighty deeds and a plan for a brave new world.

But the plan was already disintegrating. Canada did not manage to scrape together the money to become a partner in the project, which at first had been estimated at a total cost of forty-three million dollars, and later a hundred million.

"The project really depended on the Canadians' cooperation and financial support," Sumner Pike, a former member of the Atomic Energy Commission and a native of eastern Maine, recalled not long ago. "But there was a lot of opposition to Quoddy in Canada, especially from the fisheries people. Some biologists had the idea that Passamaquoddy Bay was what they liked to call 'a big mixing bowl.' All the currents and tides and rivers were supposed to carry in the nutrients twice a day, don't you know, and mix them all up, and so it was a fantastic nursery.

"Well, those ideas have been modified now," Pike went on.

"But in those days the Canadian fishing industry, which is very powerful, threw its weight against a Quoddy project. The industry dominates the politicians, and being elected to the Canadian Senate just amounts to getting a free license to lobby."

As Canada's interest waned, opposition mounted south of the border, too. Republicans began calling the project a vast boondoggle. The private utilities, having lost Muscle Shoals to TVA, were in full cry against Quoddy. Maine's Republican governor, who had promised to get the state to create an "Authority" to take over the power project when it was completed, began to drag his feet. (Such an authority was provided for because it was generally believed to be unconstitutional for the federal government to sell electric power.) Congressmen, under pressure from the power interests and Roosevelt-haters, cut back the needed funds, and in 1936 Quoddy was allowed to die. In the autumn of that year Maine joined Vermont in voting against the New Deal.

And so eastern Maine, ignored by the outside world, turned in on itself. Shipbuilding and the fisheries further declined. Eastport's twelve sardine canneries shrank to two; its population, which stood at 5300 in 1900, shrank to 2550 in 1960 and to below 2000 in 1970. A New England exodus was nothing new, of course. For over a century young men had been leaving to make their careers in the West (and even in the South: Simon Legree, remember, was a Vermonter). But now the pace had accelerated.

And what was left behind? Some bold and independent people, of course. Lobstermen still rode out of Machiasport, Jonesport, Cutler, Winter Harbor and the other eastern Maine ports on sturdy little boats, often built with their own hands. The men cut pulpwood in the forests, dug clams and marine worms on the mud flats, and made ends meet in their village grocery stores, garages, and boatyards. The women packed sardines and blueberries in the local "factories," wove balsam wreaths at Christmastime, and worked for "people from away" in the summertime. And all around them remained the clean water and fresh air and magnificent views and a variety of living things that their fathers had known but that had disappeared from the lives of most Americans.

And, scarcely noticeable, there began a countermigration by people who were groping for a world that seemed to have been lost to them. Ada and I became a part of that countermigration.

3

THE
COMMUNITY

WE SETTLED into our new home on the cove. It did
not seem likely that we could remain away much
longer from the source of my income in Manhattan, though
for the moment we were so pleased with our surroundings that
we gave the future little thought. I was in no hurry to be
reabsorbed into the fringes of that New York literary scene
where the successful writer is the one who is best able to get the
public to buy his particular neurosis. Our agreement with the
Hardings was to rent the camp for fifty dollars a month,
without a lease. We paid the electricity bill for the lights,
stove, and refrigerator. We heated the place with wood in a
small Franklin stove.

The camp, as I have said, was most unprepossessing, its frail
boards painted white with a blue trim and roofed with
brick-colored shingles enclosing two rooms. Part of the bedroom had been partitioned to create a cubicle that contained a
toilet and a basin. Although we had running water, there was

no tub or shower; sponge baths or the frigid cove rendered us fit for nice society.

From the front windows we looked out on the cove, and then to the wooded islands beyond, which stood between us and the open sea. A half-dozen other camps, all of sturdier build than our flimsy shelter, were set down here and there along the cove's sickle-shaped shoreline. Behind us a grass clearing stretched to the dirt road, and there were mixed spruce and hardwood trees densely grown up on the other side of it.

Several skiffs were anchored where the sandy beach in front of the camp graded into mud flats. These skiffs belonged to a few sometime-lobstermen who used them to row out to the slightly larger boats they had moored in the channel outside the cove and in which they tended their traps. One of the lobster fishermen asked us if he could leave his car next to ours when he went out in his boat. He was a good-looking man in his fashion, fortyish, with a finely modeled head and a shock of hair whose color gave him his nickname, Goldie, but his grin bared only the discolored stubs of the few teeth he had left. It cannot be said that he practiced any trade methodically. He dug enough clams in the summer and cut enough pulpwood in winter for his family to scrape by on.

"I make just about enough hauling my traps to pay for my gasoline," he told me one day. "But it gives us some lobsters to eat."

For a time Goldie went to vocational school to learn a trade that would give him a place in "modern society." But he didn't stick to it, and pretty soon he was back cheerfully tending his traps and digging his clams. The lobsters he didn't need for his family's sustenance he kept in a crate, or "car," moored in the channel until he had collected enough of them to sell to the local dealer. He told me to row out anytime and help myself, at fifty cents apiece. On most days we did away with the customary soup-and-sandwich lunch and threw a couple of lobsters in the pot.

When we arrived it was not very likely we would become a functioning part of the community, any more than we had in Fiesole, Innsbruck, or Arles. At first we made few friends our own age in the community; childless, we were not part of the young parents' crowd with their pressing personal concerns, and our economic ties lay elsewhere. Most of our friends, in fact, were old people. In recent years we have probably attended more funerals in a nonprofessional capacity than anyone else our age in the country.

Let me describe the community. Like Machias and other coastal towns in this part of the state, it was a pre-Revolutionary settlement on a millstream. Sawmills rose along the river. Its marshes were impounded behind dikes, and the rich hay that was cut from them was sent upriver to feed the hundreds of horses that were needed during the winter in logging operations. The town became a prosperous shipbuilding center during the nineteenth century, with its ships sailing all over the world and coastal schooners putting into its docks. By 1890 the population had reached a peak of around 2000. Then it leveled off, dropping steadily toward the 1100 people who live here today. Some towns have a ready explanation for a static population: "Every time a baby is born here," so the story goes, "a young man leaves town." For our community the explanation is better documented and it can be found in the Town Clerk's Report. For 1970, a typical year, the report read: "Births – 13, Deaths – 26."

Here are some more statistics for the same year. The town paid $81,914.14 to the school administration district to educate its children, and appropriated $27,827 to finance the rest of its own business. Of this sum, $1000 went to the Police Department ($45.54 was returned unused at the end of the year), $200 to Civil Defense (all of it was returned), $25 for the Washington County Chamber of Commerce, and $500 for the Town Poor (the optimistic town fathers went into the hole to the tune of $1787.83 on that one). Aside from schools and town salaries, the largest single expenditure was for snow removal, which came to $6572.36.

The town does not handle *all* the vital appropriations. Recently the local Chamber of Commerce jumped into the breach to pay for a new Santa Claus suit. The old one had been badly scuffed the year before when Santa, after handing out candy to the town children from the rear of the fire engine, indulged himself with his own Christmas cheer and fell off his perch.

The romantic era of sail is nearly forgotten. (Today there are hardly any leisure sailboats to be seen on the bay; the people who were born here simply do not sail in salt water, and most yachtsmen apparently do not like to cross the bar at Petit Manan Point, which separates the Bar Harbor region from Washington County waters.) What, then, sustains the community? Commerce, for one thing. As a tourist approaches town on U.S. Route 1 he is informed by a large sign that he is about to enter THE SHOPPING CENTER OF WESTERN WASHINGTON COUNTY. He will find the usual assortment of business places that line the streets of any town this size in Maine—three or four groceries, a dry-goods store, a gift shop, a drugstore, and an ice-cream joint where the kids hang out. But what really make this "the shopping center" are a state liquor store and Frankenstein's.

The liquor store is important to the town. People who live some miles distant in Washington and Hancock Counties and who might otherwise shop closer to home are lured to our town by the opportunity to pick up their week's liquor supply with their other purchases. There is no other liquor store for thirty miles on either side, and thus the local people consider themselves fortunate. The state's decision to place a liquor store here was based on considerations other than geography, however, though the man chiefly responsible doesn't like to brag about it in this rather "conservative" town.

David J. Kennedy, sometimes called "the most powerful man in Maine" during his tenure as Speaker of the state's

House of Representatives, is the town druggist. He is a short, dark-haired man in his middle sixties, with a round face into which he habitually sticks a cigar. As a young businessman, Kennedy encountered the reforms of Franklin D. Roosevelt and the New Deal and never quite recovered from them. He examines both his friends and each new piece of legislation for traces of "socialism," and though we are on the best of terms he thinks he has uncovered a suspicious strain in some of my spoken and written comments. When I arrive at the polling place on Election Day, I often find Dave seated there on a camp chair, chewing his cigar and looking over the voters.

"Well, Frank," he will growl, "I'm sorry we don't have any Socialist candidates for you on the slate today."

Kennedy's career has followed the classic course of the small-town, self-made businessman who rises to power in state politics.

"I was always interested in government and involved in town affairs," Kennedy told me once. "I've gone through all the chairs—I started in as a member of the school committee, and then I was an assessor, and then I got well-known enough so that I ran for the board of selectmen. We had a very bad system of town government by the selectmen for many years—in those days the selectmen were elected from the welfare rolls. We had a very high welfare cost in this town back in the 1940s and those people dominated the town government. I helped to change all that by having the town-manager form of government created here."

After his oldest son returned from college to take over the drugstore, Kennedy was able to run for the state legislature and spend part of the year at Augusta. One of his most important services to the town was his active support of a bill to add ten new liquor stores throughout the state. On the House floor he defended the bill against the Representative from Ellsworth, which had the only liquor store in the area at that time and wanted to keep it that way. "I couldn't see why our people had to drive thirty miles to buy a bottle of whisky,"

Kennedy said. Partly as a reward for Kennedy's support, the State Liquor Commission awarded his home town one of the new stores and thus ensured its commercial leadership among the other small towns in the area.

Frankenstein's, a department store, is something else again. Bob Whitten, its founder, was an exception in an area where little emphasis is placed on hoopla. Whitten originally ran the local franchise for the Ben Franklin Stores chain. When he severed the connection, so the story goes, he did not want to spend any more money than necessary in replacing the big sign over the entrance, so he came up with a name—Frankenstein's—that would make use of most of the letters left over from the old sign. He pressed the new association to his advantage. His paper bags soon appeared with likenesses of the monster printed on them, and a Bangor television station began to feature a late-night amateur hour sponsored by Frankenstein's, with exhortations to "come visit the friendly monster." In recent years the startled villagers have found themselves bumping into little people all over town at Christmastime. These, too, were Whitten imports, members of a troupe of dwarfs he had collected to appear in an extravaganza entitled "Santa and His Elves." Bob Whitten died in 1971, taking some of the town's color with him, but no one has yet driven a stake through the monster's heart.

Otherwise, life goes on in Yankee fashion:

Old men of less teeth than tongue still drop into the barbershop every morning to read the communal copy of the *Bangor Daily News* and thus save thirteen cents.

A local clam dealer finds that he cannot fill his quota of orders because the diggers simply quit work when they figure they have earned enough money for that particular week. The dealer solves the problem by lowering the price he pays for clams; the men grumble but dig more clams to earn their own notion of a week's pay, and the dealer fills his quota.

A woman haggles with Phil Sawyer, who operates the Chrysler franchise, over the price of a used car. She threatens to take her trade to Ellsworth, thirty miles away, but Sawyer stands firm. "Oh, well," the woman says at last. "Why should I go all the way to Ellsworth when I can get screwed right here in town?"

The community's industrial life, as we shall see, is carried on spasmodically, with women playing a role more prominent than that found in American industry as a whole at any time since the heyday of Rosie the Riveter. These industries, chiefly the packing of sardines and blueberries and the manufacture of Christmas wreaths, are seasonal. Wages generally approximate whatever legal minimum happens to be in force at the time.

Nature's bounty is harvested on a less commercial basis, too. Visitors from New York or Boston, and even from larger towns in Maine, are amazed by the high cost of groceries; transportation difficulties and the lack of serious competition with the one supermarket in town account for the prices. In their spare time men supply their families with a balanced diet by fishing for trout, striped bass, mackerel, and Atlantic salmon (ours is one of the few Atlantic salmon rivers left in North America, pollution having helped to wipe out the species elsewhere) and by digging clams; mussels, on the other hand, are considered fit fare only for the gulls. More exotic items are goose-grass greens and moose-meat mincemeat, both as satisfying on the tongue of the linguist as on that of the gourmet; the greens are gathered along the shore, while the moose meat is provided either by poachers or by hunting parties who travel to Canada, where moose hunting is legal in season. Ducks, too, are shot in season—and out. In fact, one hails the advent of the duck-hunting season not by remarking that it is about to open but that "the fine comes off tomorrow."

Hunting is far and away the most popular sport here; the bay's water is too cold for pleasurable swimming and the playing or watching of games is usually considered kid stuff. Here the rod-and-gun magazines (cover photo of up-rearing, slavering grizzly) replace in suggestion and spirit the homosexual magazines (cover photo of a comely young man smiling mockingly and flexing his enormous biceps) that are displayed on newsstands in the cities. When the deer-hunting season opens, at the start of November, half the businesses in town shut down. The barber and the plumber go off into the woods for a week or so and those in need of their professional services simply wait it out. One of my friends here is a kindly old man who, nevertheless, believes there is something degenerate about a man who doesn't own a gun. So boundless is his good will that he never suspects me (or anyone else, probably) of this deficiency and thus we get along fine.

One morning I happened to mention to him that I had seen a rabbit in front of my house.

"Did you shoot it?" he asked eagerly.

"No. Why should I shoot it?"

"Because it eats all the vegetables," he said.

Some weeks later I told him I had seen a fox near the house.

"Did you shoot it?" he demanded.

"No. Why should I shoot it?"

"Because it eats all the rabbits," he said.

4 BECOMING A PART OF THE PROBLEM

SOON AFTER we had settled in our new home I had to drive to New York to find free-lance writing assignments that would replenish our shrunken savings, and we became acquainted with the kindness of our neighbors. The camps near us in the cove were owned by people who lived the year round somewhere in the area, or who had been born here and returned from other places to spend the summer. During the week I was away they kept an eye on Ada, brought her groceries from town, presented her with homemade pies, took her on short excursions through the countryside, and in general made her feel very much at home.

Somehow, in the midst of all this attention, Ada found time to embark on a project of her own. While reading *The Farmer's Almanac* one day, she came upon a recipe for dandelion wine. The lawns around the various camps nearby were ablaze with golden blossoms, so she diligently picked every one and threw them into the pot with the other ingredients called for in the recipe. It was only when she had bottled the stuff and stored it away that a neighbor told her that the flowers she had picked were hawkweeds, not dandelions. (We found hawkweed wine not half bad on a bitter winter evening.)

The incident pushed us back to our guidebooks. We began to brush up on our botany (noting first that dandelions have a fleshy, hollow stem, the similarly colored hawkweeds a narrower, solid stem) and learned the names of the northern wild flowers that grew around us. Soon the succession of these plants took their place for us in the fascinating rhythm of the tides and the migrations of birds that bound us to this new world.

After more than two years in Europe, I began to pick up once more the study of American birds. Every morning, in fog or sun, I walked along the dirt road or down the partly overgrown logging roads that ran into it, watching and listening. The most challenging part now was to try to match new songs with the birds I already knew by sight. I remember that John Kieran once said that he did ninety per cent of his bird "watching" by ear, and I saw how much more I apprehended of the woods when I could identify even the creatures that were hidden from me by curtains of leaves and brush.

Another revelation here was the arrival in late summer of the shore birds—those mottled sandpipers and plovers that flew to Arctic regions for their brief nesting seasons and then trailed back in enormous flocks to their wintering grounds in warmer climates. And one day near the camp I saw a small bird rise and fly away at my approach, revealing flashing white tail feathers as it disappeared. I thought there was something familiar about it. I tracked it down and, after a good look at it, realized that it was the towhee, one of the first birds I had identified during our summers at Fire Island. But the small paperback publication on Maine birds that I consulted said that the towhee was confined to southwestern Maine. Had I stumbled on a rarity? I wrote to the Maine Audubon Society at Portland, and received a reply thanking me for my report, encouraging me to deliver regular reports on birds in eastern Maine, where there was a shortage of bird watchers, and admitting that the publication I had consulted was slightly out of date; in recent years the towhee had been extending its range Down East. I have that adventurous towhee to thank for leading me into my first contact with the Audubon Society.

But for the moment the shore-bird flocks and migrating towhees bore a more pertinent message. Fall was advancing, and winter bearing down. Was it time to leave Maine? After all, this still wasn't home to us, we were still "strangers" to Maine, as we would always be "the people from away" to all the natives in the town. Hadn't the summer really been a part of our long trip, the cove here just another link with the Dutch freighter, Antwerp, Fiesole, Innsbruck, and the farm in Provence in that itinerary that had begun nearly three years before with our flight from the city? Since then we had carried our world with us. We had established our own autonomous state wherever we had settled down, with our books, our typewriters, and even our teapot, whose shininess had mirrored each of those remembered settings so that when it fell and smashed one day Ada said that it seemed a part of those Old World settings had smashed too.

Here on the Maine coast our deepening ties with the natural world were beginning to impose form on our experience. Every change in the wind, every pulsation of the tide, every step in the procession of life at the cove, had struck a responsive chord in us, though we had not sent down roots. We were still "summer people." It would require something on our part (some kind of surrender, perhaps?) to weld us to the country.

We took the first step in that direction late in October. Ben and Ida Mae Harding, our landlords, came from Thomaston to visit us and make a proposition.

"We'd like to have somebody in this place year round," Ben said. "I'd put an oil burner in the big room and charge you only ten bucks a month rent. Why don't you stay the winter?"

Why not? We couldn't beat the price, that much was certain. Our money had nearly run out in Europe and I had earned very little money since our return to the United States. By moving back to New York we would be able to solve that, of course. I had already received an offer to go to work as a writer-editor on a well-paying magazine in the city, and I knew I could make a comfortable living there as a free-lance writer, too. But, overriding every other consideration, neither of us wanted to live in or near the city any more. The necessity to move to "better oneself" had always puzzled me. How often had I heard someone say, "I don't want to move, I want to stay where I am, but how can I turn down an offer like this?" I have never been able to understand why, when a man and his family are happy and reasonably well off, they must pull up stakes and move on to a place they find disagreeable simply because it represents a "promotion" or "more security." More often than not they spend the rest of their productive years yearning to retire and return to the place where they had been happy. I don't call that "security," I call it self-destruction.

And so we committed ourselves to a winter in the cove. In a sense the urge to "test" ourselves under unusual circumstances may have played a part in our decision, though only superficially. I have never been a masochist. In any case, the rigors at the cove would amount to little more than fetching one's own wood and water and coping with leaks and drafts. The chief lure was an opportunity to watch winter's progress in comparative isolation.

The people who had summered in the nearby camps had all returned to their winter homes. Our only neighbors on the peninsula were Clarence and Hazel Bagley, who lived half a mile up the road. Joe Stevens, the town's retired postmaster who owned the camp next to the one we were living in, paid us frequent visits but doubted that we could survive with nothing but ill-fitted, uninsulated boards between us and a Maine winter. He offered to put us up in a relative's house in town

"for nothing." On the other hand, Goldie, the sometime-lob-
sterman, said he didn't think we'd have any trouble. (I might
have doubted his estimate had I known where he lived: it was
the only house I have ever seen where the chimney was held
up by a rope fastened to the outside walls.) Meanwhile, we
banked the camp with tarpaper and evergreen boughs,
plugged up as many of the leaks as possible, and accepted the
loan of an old buffalo robe from a lady in town who had used
it once upon a time to bundle herself in during open-sleigh
rides and which we spread between bedsprings and mattress to
keep out the drafts that swirled unendingly across the camp's
floor. Since water came to the camp through shallow pipes it
had to be shut off against the frost; I left an ax at the spring in
the woods so I could chop a hole in the ice when I went there
to fill my water buckets. We were ready for winter's onset.

—

"*November 17, 1961*—A warm (50s) rainy day at the cove,
clearing briefly in the afternoon and closing with clumps of
'fog blossoms' drifting in from the sea. As I walked to the
spring I nearly stepped on the nuthatches, a dozen of which
were hopping over the moss and pine needles searching for
food. Other nuthatches in the trees blew their toy trumpets at
me. Joe Stevens visited his camp here this afternoon. He found
a rat in a trap he had set inside. We chatted with Joe for a
while. He told us he's had the same screen door on his camp
for 30 years, while the screens on other camps rot out and must
continually be replaced. The reason—his is *inside* the front
door and so is protected from the salt spray.

"Tonight I unpacked some of the books we brought back
with us from storage. I don't own any land, so books are the
only possessions I take pride in. I came across a copy of
Hemingway's short stories that my father had sent me when I
was in the Navy. Apparently the book had followed me all
over the Pacific, sitting sometimes in damp island depots, for
when it caught up with me its cover was mildewed and its
pages discolored. Turning those pages tonight I thought about

the war for the first time in a long while. This damaged book, and a few others I carried in my seabag, are the only souvenirs of the war I kept. I'll reread all of them this winter.

"*Dec. 3*—The fine weather continues, 26 degrees at 8 a.m., but there was a warm sun and blue skies. I sawed wood, Ada blacked the Franklin stove and stovepipe, and we tacked plastic storm coverings to the windows outside. In the evening we went to the movies in town (REST ROOMS CLOSED FOR THE WINTER, a sign in the lobby read).

"Back at the camp we lit a fire in the Franklin stove— nearly a fatal mistake. First the stovepipe began to smoke, then it burst into flames. I threw a bucket of water up at it and the flames went out. Perhaps the stoveblack contained alcohol and burned off quickly, like the brandy on a fruitcake. It was a scare, but no damage was done, except that a clay tablet bearing the inscription GOD BLESS OUR HOME broke in the confusion.

"*Dec. 4*—One of the most beautiful mornings yet; 28 degrees at 8 a.m., a blue sky and a hot sun. The proportion of fine days seems much greater now than in the summer, when the fogs come rolling in. We could hear and distinguish a large flock of old-squaw ducks honking far out on the bay. Goldie has taken in all of his traps. In the afternoon we drove to the lobster pound and bought three lobsters for dinner ($3\frac{1}{2}$ pounds at 50 cents a pound). A man there said this was about the end of the lobsters around our bay until spring. He had put up his boat two days ago because there is no real harbor here and the fresh-water ice comes down the river and cuts up the boats.

"*Dec. 10*—A gray but warm day (34 degrees). It was as if the buffleheads knew the hunting season had ended yesterday, for there was a flock of 20 or 30 in the cove all morning. At the spring I saw a flock of a dozen crossbills. I remember reading in Europe that their bills were distorted by their struggle to pull the nails from Our Savior's hands and feet. Their bills are good for extracting the seeds from spruce cones, too.

"The radio that Joe Stevens loaned us has broken down. He

said we should have a radio to check on storm warnings, but we hardly ever turned it on. It's been a long time since I needed to learn about news as it 'breaks.' The *Bangor News* will tell me about it tomorrow, or *Time* will tell me next week. I am reading a history of the Hapsburg Monarchy as background for the children's book I plan to write about Austria. Some of Metternich's doings are big news to me, and I can wait to be fascinated by the latest drama in the life of General de Gaulle, too.

"*Dec. 24*—After a series of incredibly blue, windless days, this morning broke gray. We picked up our Christmas turkey in town. At 9:30 the snow and wind arrived, and they have been rushing across the cove ever since. Tonight the storm howls around the camp, here and there a little snow gets in, and though we have the oil burner high we can feel the cold underfoot.

"*Dec. 25*—All night long the wind rocked the camp, tearing at it first from the northeast, then shifting to the northwest. We felt as if we were in a storm at sea. The wind tore off one of the plastic storm windows and carried it into the bay; it returned on the tide this morning. The snow continued almost 24 hours, the wind sculpting it into gracefully rounded mounds and knife-edge cavities. Behind the camp the grass is visible in spots, while in front the drifts lie four feet high. All along the front of the camp enormous icicles hang from the eaves, so that to look out the window is to have the sensation of being in a cage.

"To dress, fight my way up the hill through drifts sometimes waist high, fill my buckets, and return to the camp took me two hours (it was foolish not to have had snowshoes here). The spring lay under six inches of slush, which I first spooned out with a bucket. Afterward we brought in snow and melted it on the oil burner to augment our water supply.

"The snow stopped at 9 a.m., and the sun shone the rest of the day. At four o'clock Clarence Bagley came down the road on his horse to see if we were all right. He said I could ride the horse into town if I needed anything there. But a little later the town plow arrived and we were able to drive into town to wish our families 'Merry Christmas' by phone. We ate our turkey at dark."

—

It was settled for us. The winter that began on Christmas Eve marked out the course of our future. On this remote coast, I found all of the strands that fed my imagination. A sense of my country's past emanated from this place, not from its art or architecture (which were generally nondescript at best) but from the daily routines of people clinging stubbornly to ancient livelihoods. Deeper still there was the sense of getting in touch with something primal; not a "wilderness," surely, as backpackers pursue in the Western mountains, but a land-scape whose inhabitants have not yet knocked off the hard edges. This stage was not irreparably scarred, nor was it ornamental. The sea that pulsed in and out of the bays and coves brought herring in its flow or, receding, uncovered the rich mud flats for clam diggers and shore birds. Life was attuned to this polar complexity. Here was a world I could *touch*, and that *touched* me, where I could "feel the earth as rough to all my length." Here in my own country was a place that still confronted the world with a personality. Here was a place with a sense of *place*.

With a small down payment and a generous mortgage (the bank apparently felt we had struck a good bargain) we bought a home of our own, an old farmhouse on a hill overlooking the wide bay. The break with our past was not complete, of course, for we had neither the skills nor the desire to go "back to nature." I remained in touch with publishers and editors in New York. After all, the big city was only five hundred miles away, a short hop by air from Bangor, when I needed to go for research, interviews, conferences, and the other business to which a free-lance writer is tied. Ada, who held a degree in education from Hunter College, could teach in the local schools to carry us over the lean periods (which, at first, were long and frequent). We became citizens of Maine.

For most of our married life Ada and I had lived on the edge of the "system," either in New York or in Europe. We had found ourselves increasingly identifying with the footloose young people of the 1950s—the disaffected students, the pale-faced young women with stringy dark hair who no longer believed it glamorous to work as typists and receptionists on Madison Avenue, the bearded dropouts who lived in lofts and dressed like one of their own collages. We had been repelled by the urban and suburban environments, distrustful of their values, bored by their politics.

In Maine we had found an environment that vibrated with life. The real world—the natural world—was not merely a tableau to be amused by on weekends in museums and nature reserves. It was a world to live in, to feel a part of. The succession of tides and plants and migrating birds became, *mirabile dictu,* more real than the events described in the daily newspapers. They superseded even that shadow of a shadow that passed as reality on the evening news telecast.

But something was going on out there that spread a cloud of some substance over our world. "The solution of pollution is dilution," people used to say on an uncluttered planet. Now people themselves were proliferating like cancer cells. Addicted to bigness and plenty, they had driven technology beyond its capacity to function in harmony with the environment. The people and their wastes were spilling over into the planet's backwaters, leaving indelible marks. Ada and I were, in truth, a part of that spillover, a part of the problem on the Maine coast.

There was no question now of "preserving" that place we had blundered into as it once was, for the planet was moving, and Maine with it. But could people like us, who saw what we had come to love now threatened from without and within, help to direct the way in which change might take place? Our problems, we saw, were essentially those that confronted every other American. Our conviction that the natural world still really matters inevitably drew us back into the community of man.

PART·TWO
Sea and Shore

5 WHERE HAVE ALL THE HERRING GONE?

![decorative] OFTEN IN THE MORNING, while I am writing, I hear a throatier roar from the bay than that uttered by passing lobster boats. Since very few large pleasure cruisers visit the local harbor, I know almost without looking up that the roar comes from one of the two sardine carriers—the *Gary Alan* and the *Lawrence Wayne*—that belong to a factory in town. They are low-slung boats, their decks piled with the bags of salt that will be poured as a preservative onto the herring in the hold. At night I see their lights as they come up the bay, probing for the channel at low water; a woman who lives on the shore in town tells me that sometimes she wakes in the night with a start to see her bedroom flooded with light, and then goes quickly back to sleep when she realizes it is only the *Gary Alan* or the *Lawrence Wayne* finding its way to its berth. There is nothing supernatural about a sardine boat on the Maine coast.

Even so, I sometimes get a queer feeling when the *Gary Alan* sails past. This stubby little craft is the stuff of which legends are made. One black midnight a few years ago as the *Gary Alan* entered the bay from the open sea, its hold filled with herring, there occurred one of those lapses that come to all professionals at one time or another. The *Gary Alan* rammed an object that was never clearly identified, filled quickly, and sank. The crew made it ashore to a nearby island with no ill effects beyond a chilling dip. But that was not the end of the *Gary Alan*. It was hauled up from the shallow water where it had sunk, pumped out, and towed to a boatyard on Mount Desert Island. There the rust was scraped from its vitals and fresh paint slapped on its hull. Now it is back in service with its sister ship, its light probing the bay on dark nights with somewhat more diligence.

It would be nice to think of the *Gary Alan*'s saga as an omen of things to come in the local sardine industry. Like much else in Washington County, the industry has gone on the rocks in recent years but it will require more than a bit of scraping and painting before it is restored to the ranks of the quick. Sardines have been basic here for a long time. Lobster fishing, of course, provides the glamour, with its practitioners (lobstetricians?) standing for good old Down East independence in an era of "creeping socialism," and its artifacts set about the landscape, quaintly, like rosy-cheeked angels on a baroque ceiling. But it's a man's game—and a capitalist's one, at that. (Even on a modest scale, the initial investment is high; a friend of mine, who had been helping another lobster fisherman but wanted to go out on his own, managed to wheedle a four-thousand-dollar loan from the bank to buy the old wooden boat and 250 traps of another man who was about to retire.)

The business of catching sardines and putting them in cans touches more of the community. Among the town's less well-to-do, some of the women are able to provide a substantial share of the family income because of the sardine industry. If the herring are reasonably abundant and the factory (or cannery) open a good deal of the time, then the women will have compiled enough working hours to qualify for state unemployment compensation during the off season. During winters when this supplement is not available to the women, cash is in short supply and IOUs pile up at the expense of the hard-pressed local merchants.

The arrival of a boat loaded with herring sets off the factory's whistle and stirs the town to action. The women who pack the herring (the young of the *Clupea harengus*) in cans as "sardines" rush to the factory, or are picked up and taken there by the management's bus. It is easy to spot a woman who is on her way to pack fish: her hair is bound in a net, she carries the scissors with which she will slice open the fish, and her fingers are likely to be swathed in bandages, for more than herring are sliced when a woman is paid by piecework and her income depends on the number of cans she is able to pack in a given time. It is hard, dirty, smelly work, tempered by an opportunity to socialize.

"I packed sardines for a while after I first got married," a young woman in town told me. "My husband was away all day, and it gave me a chance to spend some time with my old friends. Course, the money came in handy, too."

I asked her about the scissors she used.

"Oh, you bought your scissors right there at the fish factory," she said. "They cost six dollars, but they were made of good steel and they always had somebody right there to keep them sharp for you. I've still got my scissors, though I haven't used them on fish for years. They're a nice size—not too big, and I still use them for dressmaking."

"You didn't need a knife to clean the fish?"

"No, you don't clean herring when you're packing them for sardines. They go in the can, guts and all. You'd just stand there at the tray—it was stainless steel—that they assigned you, and there were two conveyor belts that went past. The fish came by on one of them. You grabbed a fish off the belt and snipped off its head and sometimes its tail and stuffed them down the chum hole at one end of your tray. They sell the heads to the lobster fishermen to bait their traps with.

Then you'd take a can off the top conveyor belt and pack it with the fish."

"How many fish in a can?"

"Oh, it seems like you'd get fifteen or twenty of the nice little ones in a can, though maybe not as many as that. But those big fish, you could pack only three or four in. Didn't I hate to pack those big ones! They were awful hard on your hands."

But today the Maine sardine industry is beset by a two-edged sword—a lack of both herring and profitable markets. It is a local disaster when, because of economics or fire (a recurrent event in an area where the factories are dilapidated wooden buildings), a town loses its sardine industry. The industry is an entity one is able to identify with, as Ada and I discovered while we were on a trip through the South. We are indifferent to words of praise for the Maine lobster, because after all a lobster may have been pulled out of the water at any point along our coast or, indeed, it may be a Maine lobster in name only, hailing from some grimy bay to the west'ard. But one day we were shopping in a small grocery store in Florida's panhandle when all our latent boosterism was stirred by the sight, there on the shelf in front of us, of a stack of canned sardines bearing the label of one of our local factories. We bought two cans, and their taste (though our local sardines are hardly gourmet items) called up visions of the Maine coast far more vividly than a "Maine" lobster might have done under the same circumstances.

Maine's flourishing sardine industry sometimes packed three million cases in a good year. When the total dropped to one million cases a few years ago, it was said that hard times had arrived; but in 1971 a Washington County canner estimated that only four hundred thousand cases were packed along the entire coast. Lubec, in the county's eastern corner, reflects the coast's herring disaster: nearly a dozen canneries once operated in the area, now only two survive—and both are in trouble. Compounding Lubec's troubles was the announcement in 1971 by the American Can Company that it would shut down its can-manufacturing plant there, putting more than forty people (with a payroll of a quarter of a million dollars) out of work. The company simply had no one to sell cans to any more in eastern Maine. The loss of the company will be felt in a variety of other ways. It paid thirty thousand dollars in annual taxes to the town and twelve thousand in fees to the local water-and-light district. Since transportation costs to this isolated area are high (one of the other reasons for the can manufacturer's departure), the local sardine factories will be put to greater expense in the future when they must import cans from other parts of the country to pack their fish in.

Still, the scarcity of fish is causing the most acute hardship. The boats seldom find large schools of herring offshore. The bays along the coast used to bristle with weirs—large underwater "corrals" constructed of nets fastened to posts or cut saplings, where herring are lured and trapped. Schools of young herring no longer frequent the bays, and the weirs are disappearing; during the early 1960s there were seventeen profitable herring weirs in Machias Bay, but by the 1970s there were none. In 1971 the owner of a large sardine factory in Jonesport reported that he had on hand enough fish to pack only sixty-five thousand cases, one-fourth his normal total. At this factory only six of the fastest women workers (among the forty-eight who packed fish there) earned the annual minimum of six hundred dollars that they needed to qualify for unemployment compensation during the winter.

"It seems like everything this part of Maine used to depend on has just dried up and disappeared," Sumner Pike, now an octogenarian, was saying not long ago in Lubec. "Everybody had a small boat and went fishing during the summer, a lot of it for haddock and cod. They split and salted them. There was a big demand for dried fish. We sent it to the West Indies and all over, because they didn't have much refrigeration in those days.

"But the biggest thing here was smoked herring. We shipped them all over, too, along with the cod and the haddock, and if you were a Catholic you *had* to eat the damn things. Then, of course, Prohibition came in and the free lunch disappeared. All the saloons in the old days offered a free lunch that was loaded with salty foods like smoked herring that made you thirsty, and so that disappeared, too."

The decline of dependable markets for herring has continued right to our own time. As the catch became uncertain and the canneries failed to fill orders from the supermarket chains, big buyers began to lose confidence in them and resorted to imported sardines and other canned goods to fill the space on their shelves. In turn, the Maine canners have tried to pad out their production by using large (and therefore rather elderly) sardines that do not compare in quality with the tasty little sardines produced by the Norwegians.

"Some of the imported cans have as much as twenty-two fish in them," a Maine canner admits, "while we seem content to pack in four big ones, which are just a mess. We get a bad name."

The trend along the Maine coast in recent years has been for a decline in landings among all species of fish. This is true even of lobsters, though the decline has been smaller and the price has risen considerably, thus staving off hard times for most lobster fishermen. But the disappearance of many other kinds of fish has been catastrophic.

I miss very little here that I prized in the city, but what I grumble about most when I go into a local grocery or supermarket is that there is no decent bread or fresh fish to be had. Once in a while a man from Lubec comes into town peddling fresh fish from a truck, though even these fish have been caught at Campobello in New Brunswick and not in Maine. Haddock, once common on the market, are now rare; a federal expert has predicted that the haddock fisheries face "total collapse." A few years ago shrimp suddenly appeared in great numbers off the Maine coast. Many local fishermen quickly converted their boats to shrimp draggers and made a lot of money. But the next year the shrimp catch was off and the fishermen suffered heavy losses.

But it is the herring that most concern eastern Maine. Herring have been declining all over the North Atlantic for some years now, and *The New York Times* reports that a catch that amounted to 1.7 million tons of herring by all nations in 1966 had dropped to 250,000 tons a couple of years later. The fish are simply not showing up on this side of the Atlantic, as they did in great numbers until very recently. Some people, both scientists and fishermen, are inclined to blame "natural cycles" or "climatic changes" for the decline, and there is historical precedent for such a belief. In *The Sea Around Us*, Rachel Carson told how a change in the relative position of the sun, moon, and earth had altered the tides off northern Europe so that their force no longer impelled the great schools of herring from the North Sea into the gateways of the Baltic; the course of history was altered as Sweden, impoverished by the decline in the herring fisheries on which she depended, relinquished the fisheries and her economic ascendency to Holland on the North Sea.

Here in eastern Maine we share a common coastline with New Brunswick. And so it was in an attempt to get an explanation for our present plight that I drove across the border not long ago to visit the Fisheries Biological Station in St. Andrews, New Brunswick. The Canadians, who have put a great deal of money into fisheries research and into subsidizing their herring fleet, take about fifty-five per cent of all the herring caught in the North Atlantic, despite the intrusion of the large fleets from Russia, Norway, West Germany, and other European nations (not to mention our own ill-equipped boats). Obviously, the Canadians share our concern as well as our coastline. I spoke to T. D. Iles, whom his colleagues at the Research Station call "Mr. Herring." Iles is a stocky man in middle age, with a pleasant face and a ready laugh.

"It is sheer madness to assume anything else but over-fishing," Iles told me. "The herring fisheries have gone steadily downhill in recent years."

"Some people say it could be a natural fluctuation," I reminded him.

Iles grimaced impatiently. "I know. We've even got people in our own department who say that, but it's nonsense. I don't deny there are natural changes that sometimes cause the herring to move. Still, the herring form huge shoals so there's no problem in finding them. If the herring have gone someplace else we'd know about it. The truth is that there are no large unexploited stocks of herring left in the North Atlantic."

"What about pollution?"

"It's not helping, that's for sure." He nodded. "We think pollution is causing problems with marine animals of all kinds, especially close to shore and in estuaries. But there's no proof yet that it's seriously affecting offshore populations."

"So everybody is just being stubborn and not facing facts?"

Iles laughed, apparently at human nature and not my naïveté. "Oh, the experts from the different countries get together and they do the best they can, but they're faced with solidly entrenched attitudes, both scientific and political. Take the Russians, for instance. They claim that it's the Canadians and the Americans who are causing the problem by catching all the juvenile herring close to shore and not giving them a chance to grow up. So we're depriving the *Russians* of fish!"

"Well, what *about* the Canadians?" I asked him.

Iles opened one of the Research Station's reports and slid it across the desk to me. There, among the statistics and the tables, was the story:

The Canadian Atlantic herring fishery increased fivefold during the 1960's. This rapid expansion was accompanied by a change from the traditional fixed-gear operation using weirs, traps and gillnets for food and bait herring to one dominated increasingly by highly mobile purse-seine fleets serving a new meal and oil industry. . . . The most fundamental biological principle is that no herring resource is unlimited in size nor inexhaustible. . . . Fishing can reduce population size more quickly, and to relatively low levels, than it does for any other species because herring school in such dense concentrations. The decline of particular herring fisheries may be so rapid that fishermen tend to attribute it to some natural calamity, unable to accept that fishing can have such a quick and drastic effect. . . . Environmental changes which result in abnormally poor year classes can indeed accelerate the decline of a fishery. This does not mean that fishing is not the major factor involved.

"Sounds grim," I said.

He nodded again. "For a long time some of our people here thought that nothing could really wipe out the herring. One herring, you know, carries an enormous number of eggs—a hundred thousand or more—so the theory was that no matter how many we took, the herring could quickly rebuild their populations. But there hasn't been a big year class of herring on the Georges Bank since 1961. We're not giving them a *chance* to spawn, so in effect we're eating our own seed corn. The question is, has the adult stock been reduced so that now it's *incapable* of producing a big year class?"

"A lot of our fish processing plants are closing down in Maine," I said. "What's all this meant to you?"

"Well, when we increased our fleet and then increased the catch, we went a bit wild in building processing plants—for canning sardines, grinding them up into fish meal, and so on. Right now the Atlantic Provinces have the plant capacity to process ten thousand tons of herring a day—enough for the whole world! Now some of the plants are closing down."

"What do you do with all the herring you catch? Canadians don't eat it all."

"It's a funny thing. It used to be a two-way street between the States and Canada. We'd ship you some herring when you needed extra supplies, and you'd ship us some. Now it's all one way, from us to you. All of the herring that's processed here in Canada is for food, including huge amounts of meal for American chickens. But in the States you people grind up huge additional amounts for fertilizer, or even use them in special industries—like those pearl-essence plants in Eastport, which use herring scales to make costume jewelry and other products. Herring that's used for purposes like that are usually too big or too little to can as sardines, so they're sold much cheaper."

"So the fishermen take all the babies for pearl essence, and they don't grow up to spawn or become sardines?"

"Right. They're almost given away at that stage. So what's happening in effect is that the fishery is being overexploited in terms of a natural resource, but underexploited economically."

"And what are you going to do about it all?"

"Well, for one thing we've made an agreement with the state of Maine that you might say will force each of us to keep our nose clean. Maine has had restrictions on the sizes of herring that could be taken—nothing smaller than four and a half inches, nothing larger than seven inches. In your country the individual states make their own fishing laws, but in Canada it's the federal government that makes the law, and they've come to an agreement with Maine to work within those limits. This may hurt the fertilizer factories, but it may help to save the fishery."

Beyond this local agreement stands the possibility of international treaties over the question of offshore waters. Decisions will be made on the highest levels. Maine's sardine industry, like the fishing industry all over New England, has slipped out of its own hands and will rise or fall because of decisions taken in Washington, Ottawa, London, Oslo, Bonn —and Moscow.

6

THE
"WILY FOX"

I DOUBT THAT many men and women who live in
eastern Maine and depend on the sea's harvest for
their livelihood have heard of the *Wily Fox*. The *Wily Fox* is a
100-foot fishing vessel owned by the Prelude Corporation of
Westport Point, Massachusetts. It sails out of New Bedford
and tends its strings of lobster traps on the fringes of the
continental shelf about seventy-five miles south of Nantucket
Island. Yet the frustrations of the men who make their living
from this vessel are simply another symptom of America's
contemporary malaise.

Early in May 1971 Captain Joseph Maillet and his crew of
the *Wily Fox* were in the midst of what a Prelude official later
called "that horrible week." Their trouble derived not from
bad weather (the weather, indeed, was mostly clear) or a
shortage of lobsters (the lobsters apparently were there in
abundance), but from the presence on their fishing grounds of
a fleet of large, beautifully equipped Russian trawlers. The
Wily Fox had already had some disagreeable encounters with

these foreign ships. One night on a previous trip it had stationed itself, with its ten thousand watts of mercury lights ablaze, between its anchored lobster gear (with seventy-five to a hundred traps on each 1200-foot trawler string) and the Russian boats. The crew of the *Wily Fox* had repeatedly blinked its lights to warn the Russians away from the lobster gear, which the Russians in the past had trawled through and destroyed. But then one of the big Russian trawlers had turned right into the brightly lighted *Wily Fox*. Only fast evasive action by its skipper had kept the *Wily Fox* from being run down.

Now, in May, the Americans were beside themselves with frustration. The *Wily Fox* had set its trawler strings in 600 feet of water, each string of traps buoyed at both ends, and clearly marked with orange "day-glo" floats, pen lights, and flags. Fishing close by was the Russian fleet, composed of at least twenty-seven vessels of two kinds—280-foot stern trawlers that fish mainly for herring and the more common side trawlers of 125 feet or more that trawl near the ocean floor for hake and mackerel. It is the side trawlers that cause most of the damage to the strings of lobster traps, dragging their gear through the Americans' complex maze of trap lines. A chart, prepared by the United States State Department in its protests to the Russians, specified some of the incidents:

APRIL 30, 1971 — The *Wily Fox* reported that approximately 18 stern trawlers at night had trawled through fixed lobster gear deployed by the *Wily Fox* resulting in the loss of 133 lobster traps and associated line and markers. The *Wily Fox* identified the vessels as Russian, based on their silhouettes and stock markings.

MAY 8, 1971 — The *Wily Fox* reported that an identified Russian fishing vessel had trawled through fixed lobster gear deployed by the *Wily Fox* with resultant damage unknown.

MAY 12, 1971 — The *Wily Fox* reported that identified Russian fishing vessels had trawled through fixed lobster gear deployed by the *Wily Fox* resulting in the loss of 122 lobster traps and associated line and markings, value estimated at $12,000.

When the crew of the *Wily Fox* hauled in its trawl lines it usually found twenty to eighty per cent of its traps had been cut and lost. Each lobster trap costs the ship's owners twenty dollars or more, and with the attendant losses of expensive trawl line, wires, clips, and anchors, the total mounted steadily. United States Coast Guard boats in the area functioned merely as observers, restrained from taking any action against the offending Soviet boats because the incidents occurred outside the twelve-mile national limit. On several occasions the *Wily Fox* pulled alongside a Soviet trawler and by shouts and hand signals indicated that the vessels were sailing over fixed lobster gear. Only once was there a response.

"Do you speak German?" the Russian skipper inquired in German.

"No," the Americans replied.

"Do you speak Russian?"

"No," the Americans said again.

"Well, I bid you good fishing," the Russian waved and the trawler went on about its business.

Sometimes the Americans saw Russian boats bring bits and pieces of lobster gear aboard. Richard A. Cooper, a marine biologist with the National Marine Fisheries Service, happened to be on the *Wily Fox* at the time, carrying out a research project on lobsters.

"On May 12," Cooper recalled, "during the latter part of the morning, we approached a Soviet side trawler that had just retrieved its outer gear. We came up on the left-hand side of the vessel, and on the roof of the wheel house I could very clearly see one of the large 'day-glo'-orange float markers with the characteristic markings that the Prelude Corporation people put on them to indicate their own gear. We made a circle around their vessel, but by the time I had my camera topside and ready to document this, one of the Soviet crew members had covered this float up."

The owners of the *Wily Fox* said that the destruction of their gear had caused their income to drop by nearly one-third during the first part of 1971; on an average trip the vessel lands twenty-three thousand pounds of lobsters, but while the Russians were in the area its hauls averaged only about ten thousand pounds.

"We have a right to be protected," Joseph S. Gaziano, the president of the Prelude Corporation told a Congressional subcommittee investigating the incidents several months later. "How can our government police the world and not protect our boats off Cape Cod? We need to extend the fishing rights off our coast to two hundred miles. If the fishing fleets of the foreign nations are going to behave like hoodlums, we should kick them out."

Official protests are made, the Russians promise to fish more carefully, and the incidents momentarily decline as the foreign fleets move on to other areas in their endless search for fish. But the conflict grows more intense with each passing year. The Coast Guard has estimated that there are between 400 and 450 large fishing boats of the Communist nations alone off the Atlantic Coast today, and they are being joined in rising numbers by Western European boats and even those of the Japanese. Similar rage-provoking incidents occur regularly on the Pacific Coast, where Russian boats run down the crab pots set out by Americans, and the Japanese and South Korean fleets increasingly take over what used to be "American" fishing grounds.

The presence of "foreign" fishing boats off our coasts is nothing new, of course. The French and Portuguese fishermen were among the earliest European visitors to North America, and their fleets have been here ever since, though until very recently there was always enough fish in the sea for everybody. Whatver conflicts and grudges arose were purely local. After

World War II the fleets of many of the world's fishing nations lay in ruins, and those of others were growing obsolete. To say that a resurgence took place would be too mild; the new technology and exploding populations have brought on a full-scale revolution in the way men harvested the sea. Ships of unprecedented size are designed and sent out to scour the oceans for protein to feed the people back home. These ships are fitted with the most sophisticated tracking, netting, and processing devices that the technicians are able to devise. The fleets remain on the sea for many months, following the schools of fish relentlessly, attended by ever larger vessels that supply the smaller ships while processing and storing their catch.

Those regions of the Old World that have been fished most heavily for generations are no longer able to supply the bulk of fish needed by Russia, Germany, Japan, and the countries of Eastern Europe. By the early 1960s these countries were dispatching their modern fleets to the rich fishing grounds off the coasts of the Americas. Colonialism, thwarted on land, has emerged in another aspect at sea.

"The Russians have an enormous fishing fleet out there, and they're scooping up everything that swims," T. D. Iles had told me in Canada. "One of their remarkable assets is that their boats are adaptable. Around 1963, for instance, there was a tremendous year class of haddock. Well, the Russians, who had been fishing mostly for herring, switched their gear so that they could go after haddock in 1965 and 1966, and they just swept them all up. We call that 'raid fishing.' Since then the haddock fishery has crashed. So the Russians switched back to herring."

Meanwhile, of all the world's great fishing fleets only that of the United States has not revolutionized itself in the last two decades. Other nations have subsidized the total renovation of their fleets, but in recent years no administration has even spent the comparatively small sums of money authorized by

Congress for boatbuilding, research, and other improvements (though these subsidies would benefit another industry, the boatbuilders, perhaps even more than the fishermen).

And so the Americans stand on the shore and shake their fists at the invaders. It might be said that we have been forced into the role of marine conservationists, for American fishing boats that once plundered the seas in their own right have been pushed into a second-rate position by their own lack of initiative and their rivals' technological ingenuity. We grumble at the Danes, who are systematically devastating the stocks of Atlantic salmon (in only seven years Greenland's exports of this prized fish rose from two metric tons to fourteen hundred metric tons). Our scientists predict that the Japanese (who were among the nations that drove whales to the edge of extinction), will now decimate the porpoises through their use of enormous nets which catch whole schools to be canned as pet food. The schools of herring, haddock, and ocean perch that once flourished off our East Coast are disappearing; the Pacific perch and the Pacific hake, the favorite targets of Russian trawlers on the West Coast, are also in trouble.

"Our two most abundant local trawl species have been heavily exploited by the Soviet Union and the Japanese," an expert in the Alaskan fisheries said recently. "We are no longer in a position to effectively establish whether or not depletion has occurred and to establish the best levels of harvest, as our fishing fleets have largely abandoned the grounds for economic and biological reasons, due to heavy importation of foreign fish. Hence, we no longer have sufficient fishing effort to gauge changes in the stock sizes."

As our own effort declines, foreign fishermen move into the vacuum. In 1971 the W. R. Grace Company announced that its SeaPak division had signed an agreement with Rumania to buy the entire production of ground fish taken by that country's new fleet of 260-foot "factory ships"; the fish will be processed at plants in Georgia and Texas. Because the demand for protein outside the United States continues to rise there is not even a chance that man's fishing pressure on the world's oceans will level off.

"At a recent international conference the Russians showed up and said they are going to have to increase their catch by *fifty per cent* in the next five years," Iles, my friend in Canadian fisheries, had told me. "Their scientists know this can't be done because the fish aren't there, but they've got to try to fish harder and harder to come close to those goals. But every country is the same. The British don't like to accept any restrictions at all on their activities—not even on dumping their wastes in the ocean—because they've been hung up for so long on their 'freedom of the seas.' Britannia rules the waves, and all that. And the West Germans made a tremendous investment in a modern fishing fleet during the 1960s. They're not about to agree to restrictions on fishing until they get their money back."

In 1938 the world's nations harvested 40 billion pounds of fish. A decade later the total had barely changed. But by 1957 the total exceeded 60 billion pounds and in recent years it has nearly *doubled* to 115 billion pounds. Yet during these three decades the production of United States fishermen remained static, so that today we import over 8 billion pounds of fish products each year, more than twice as much as we produce. Our government's various trade agreements with foreign nations help to sustain the flow of imports.

But this is the land of free enterprise, we insist, and if that is so there is no reason why the American fisherman cannot flourish by his own wit and initiative. Alas, this dying species fights odds that no other rational businessman would accept. At one time a fisherman was able to skimp on his boat and gear and get by; today he cannot compete without a substantial initial investment. Consider the case of Clifford West, a hard-working young man who fishes for lobsters out of Steuben, Maine, to support his wife and three children. He would like to replace his present 30-foot wooden boat with a larger Fiberglas boat that he could convert to fish for shrimp or scallops when the lobstering is slow.

"My brother and I built this old boat ten years ago," West said. "It cost me only seven hundred and fifty dollars, and I gave another twenty-five for a used automobile engine to put in her. The engine I got now cost me two hundred and fifty dollars over to Lewiston, but it's lasted two years, which comes out to one twenty-five a year. You couldn't run an outboard for that. I've run about five thousand gallons of gas through her, and that's a lot of mileage any way you figure it."

But recently, when Clifford West went to several local banks where his credit and reputation are good, they still refused to give him a ten-thousand-dollar loan with which to buy his new boat. A boat, so the bankers say, is a risky proposition, even in the hands of a serious young family man. West must save his money for another year or two until he scrapes together a substantial part of the boat's final cost. Then perhaps the bankers will let him have the rest.

Yet today even the fisherman who manages to get a loan from his bank finds himself strangled by its complications. An increasing number of automobile owners are learning that they can get insurance only with difficulty; the problem is even more formidable for the fisherman. A group of fishermen from Virginia stated their industry's case to a Congressional subcommittee not long ago. Insurance rates for these boat-owners increased by 100 per cent in 1970, and then went up another 250 per cent in 1971. The rates for the 110-foot trawler *Big Star* were typical. In 1968 its owners paid $13,500 in premiums to get $100,000 worth of insurance on its hull and $300,000 in protection and indemnity on its thirteen crewmen. In 1971, though the insurance companies cut the limit of their payments to $90,000 for the hull and only $100,000 for individual protection and indemnity, they asked premiums totaling $27,000.

Many boatowners would drop their insurance and trust to

their luck, but for the restrictions under which they operate. If a boat is mortgaged, the bank requires insurance on the hull; and federal law demands that the boatowners insure their crewmen against accident (in recent years the individual premiums have leaped from $500 to nearly $1500 a man). Nor are the insurance companies wholly at fault. Fishing is a hazardous business and in some areas the companies pay ninety-two cents in claims for every dollar they collect in premiums, surely a losing proposition when overhead costs are included. The vessels themselves are old and in many cases unseaworthy. Their crews are often untrained. Under the present government policies toward the fishing industry, rapid improvement is unlikely.

"To me," a government official said of remedies, "it is not unlike trying to rejuvenate slum areas of a great city by hit-and-miss repairs to collapsing and dangerous old buildings."

Ironically, even when the American fisherman manages to survive, his countrymen's attitudes put his business on a very uncertain footing. Many Catholics who always regarded fish as a penance rather than a food disdain it now that they have been released from the obligation to abstain from eating meat on Fridays. Contamination scares, like that which linked excessive amounts of mercury to swordfish, produce a drastic effect on the sales of fish. I was in New York during one of the first great pollution uproars of the early 1960s when clams from New Jersey's Raritan Bay caused an outbreak of hepatitis in the metropolitan area. Mrs. Elizabeth Wallace, the director of a shellfish trade association, pleaded for her industry's survival at a conference called by the United States Public Health Service.

"As long as these resources cannot be used," Mrs. Wallace said, "they are as a pistol to the heads of our whole industry, because should these contaminated shellfish be taken and get to the markets it destroys the industry all over our country."

To compound its problems, the industry finds itself unable

to produce a united front, even before Congress. Those fishermen who are being pushed off their traditional fishing grounds by foreign fleets cry for the United States to declare a "two-hundred-mile limit" off its coasts, within which the government will be able to establish the rules of the game. Yet those who fish for tuna or shrimp are most content with their lot today. Changing tastes in America (a tuna fish sandwich for lunch, a platter of fried shrimp for supper or late snack) have created a thriving market for those fish. However, the tuna and shrimp boats find their best fishing grounds off the coasts of those Latin American nations which claim two-hundred-mile limits of their own. So the men who run the tuna and shrimp boats want to dampen any talk about international restrictions on the high seas, while their beleaguered compatriots plead protection against the "Commie" fleets.

This sense of being put upon finds a ready response in many parts of contemporary America. Technological advances and foreign competition have changed traditional ways of life in those places, and not always for the better. The pride in our own self-sufficiency has been struck a heavy blow, and where we detect a Communist hand behind the blow all sorts of passions arise to mix with our humiliation. At one time we were our own masters; our lives were meaningful and good. We might turn to the Old World to import its frills and even its art, but in the staples of life we liked to think we stood on our own sturdy legs. What were foreigners to us but buyers for the superb and ingenious goods we produced? With what pure optimism our businessmen looked to China early in this century, dreaming of the day when 500 million "Chinamen" would clamor to buy what we had to sell—250 million automobiles, a billion rubber tires, and all those petroleum products!

The people in Maine are no different from their fellow Americans to the south and west who find themselves dancing to music that is piped by politicians, financial manipulators, or labor leaders over equally long distances. Yet these coastal people, in the throes of change, still try to find ways to carry on the independent way of life that has tied them to the sea for so many generations.

They can be very persistent about that.

7

THE WIZARDS
OF OOZE

AMONG THE FLORAL WREATHS on view at a recent funeral here was one whose attached card read: "With Deepest Regrets, from the Wormers." This description was neither a macabre joke nor a melancholy reference to man's fatuous pride. It was a simple and sincere expression of sympathy sent by a prominent segment of the community.

A wormer is a man who digs marine worms to be sold as bait. His is as noble a calling as that of the furze cutter on Egdon Heath, and far more profitable. In this area, which once sent its iron men and wooden ships all over the world, today's venturesome lad is likely to have his travels limited by the outer perimeter of the local mud flats. Nevertheless, the call still comes early. I overheard a fourteen-year-old sixth-grader gloating to an elder the other day.

"On a good day I can make twenty-five dollars digging worms," he said. "That's more'n my mother makes at the nursing home. Sure does make her mad!"

This pink and pulpy harvest helps to relieve local deficits, much as the sale of a star pitcher used to tide the old Philadelphia Phillies over a long winter. Lobster fishing is the glamour industry here, but, pound for pound, marine worms bring more cash on the wholesale market than lobsters do. The sale of worms last year brought half a million dollars into Washington and Hancock Counties. It also kept a number of people off the local welfare rolls, because it is an essentially "unskilled" trade, open to men (and even young women) who have neither the skills and temperament for more demanding employment nor the capital to try their hand at lobster fishing. To become a wormer, a man needs only a special "hoe," a bucket to drop the worms in, a pair of hip boots, access to a small boat and motor to take him to isolated mud flats, and a strong back. In addition, the serious wormer may own a light, which he clips to his cap for night digging. The light consists of a strong flashlight bulb powered by a six-volt storage battery kept in a case on his belt. It gives one a queer sensation to peer offshore on a dark night and see dozens of tiny lights bobbing up and down on mud flats that one supposed were inhabited only by herons.

Worms are thus numbered among Maine's vital natural resources, like pulpwood and seascape painters. When the weather is favorable a durable man should be able to earn two hundred dollars a week digging worms. And the labors of such men help to support their families and the local grocers in a good many depressed Maine coastal towns where the non-worming citizens frequently ride out hard times on salt cod and last year's potatoes. They also provide salt-water sport fishermen with a product they find as desirable as Maine lobsters—fresh bait.

Maine's mud flats abound in two species of commercial worms. One is the bloodworm (*Glycera dibranchiata*), a darkly mottled pink annelid, six or eight inches long, which vaguely resembles the familiar night crawler. It derives its name from the bloodlike fluid contained in its body cavity. At rest, the bloodworm's mouthparts are soft and balloon-like, but when this feature is inverted, it displays four tiny pincers. Upon piercing the human skin, the pincers inflict a sharp pain, which their victims compare to a bee sting. Though some biologists believe that the bloodworm is a vegetarian, the venom it injects in the human hand, causing a rather spectacular swelling and discoloration, suggests that it paralyzes small sea animals before devouring them. The other species is called variously the sandworm or clamworm (*Nereis virens*). Its flat body, which grows from eight to eighteen inches long (and in the latter case is called a "snake" by the wormers), is composed of a hundred or more segments. Tiny "paddles" project from the body to propel it through the water, though, like the bloodworm, it spends most of its life burrowing in the mud.

The wormers earn their money. Like Olympic swimmers, the big-money wormers burn themselves out quickly. "There was a fellow at Wiscasset who dug three thousand seven hundred and fifty worms on one tide," Clarence Bagley told me. "But one day this year they had to haul him off the flats. He just toppled over." The act of making one's way, bent at right angles from the waist, through acres of gulping mud without occasionally taking time to straighten up is, understandably, devilishly hard on backs and stomachs.

Clarence Bagley is a tall, leathery-faced neighbor who has lived off the harvest of sea and shore for most of his fifty-odd years. Since he knew I was interested in worming, he had been urging me to join him on the mud flats.

"You wouldn't write a story about cooking until you'd baked a pie, would you?" he asked.

His logic was irrefutable. I could not back out now, especially since the "trouble" recently subsided. There had been a spate of labor trouble in our area, which was unusual because this is scarcely a hotbed of Wobblies. A few years ago wormers all along the Maine coast went out on strike to get more money for their worms from the dealers. The strike was broken by the less-affluent wormers of Washington and

Hancock Counties, who could not afford to hold out for more than a couple of days. But lately our wormers have displayed more devotion to the cause. The few Down East wormers who scabbed during the recent strike found the cars they had parked near the mud flats vandalized. Some asserted that shots were fired at their persons. The more militant attitude finally prevailed, forcing the dealers to capitulate, and worm prices rose to their present all-time high—about $27.50 a thousand for sandworms, and $50 a thousand for bloods.

The morning of my appointment with Clarence broke chilly and clear. There were two young wormers with Clarence in his old station wagon when he stopped to pick me up. He drove us to the shore, where he steered the station wagon onto a stretch of hard-packed sand which had been bared by the receding tide, and then onto a rocky point. Another car, containing three wormers, was already parked there.

"You won't find any worms sitting here," Clarence called as he pulled up alongside them.

"You won't find any out there, either," one of the men in the other car said glumly.

"The worms we've been digging haven't had too much body to them," one of the young men explained. "The dealer's been complaining."

There was some small talk among the wormers as we waited for the tide to recede still further. Most of it dealt with their occupational hazards. One complained of the strain on his back, another of the high cost of the worming license, which the state had set at ten dollars.

But there seemed even more general agreement about the treachery of summer people and fogs. Access to the mud flats is limited because most of the land along the shore now is the jealously guarded property of "people from away." A man who has bought what he feels is a secluded shore lot is not likely to welcome a horde of wormers tramping over it or creating a disturbance out on the flats. Compounding these obstacles are the heavy fogs that may drift in across the flats during the night—for when the demand for bait is heavy the wormers dig two tides each twenty-four hours. The fogs often separate the wormers. A man who has neglected to bring a compass may spend some uncomfortable moments lost on the flats while the tide creeps back around him.

"When a couple of the boys get lost we begin to holler and blow our car horns from the shore," one of the wormers said. "We got into quite a row with some summer people one night for making a racket at three a.m. But I wasn't going to stop honking till we located those boys."

At a word from Clarence I got out of the car, pulled on a pair of borrowed hip boots and plodded through the sucking mud to the edge of the water where Clarence's 16-foot open boat was moored. Then we followed another wormer's boat out of the cove toward the islands in Narraguagus Bay. There was scarcely a ripple on the water. As we rode along, Clarence showed me his digging "hoe," which is really a short-handled rake with foot-long tines.

"This is a regular garden tool, with the handle cut down and an extra tine welded on each side to make six," he said. "Then an extra piece of metal is welded onto the tines to make them longer. That's because the sandworms burrow down into the mud a foot or so. That's what we got here in this bay—mostly sandworms. A man going after bloodworms would carry a hoe with *eight* shorter tines because the bloods stay near the top, but they don't gather as thick as sandworms."

Clarence said that a garage mechanic made his hoes for him, charging him about twenty dollars. Rocks and other obstacles in the mud take a fearful toll of hoes, and only the very best will serve a wormer for much more than a year. A hoe with a broken tine lay on the deck at Clarence's feet.

"Is there anything you can use the broken hoe for?" I asked.

Clarence nodded as he peered over my shoulder at the island we were approaching. "That's for you to dig with," he said.

"This looks like nice wormy ground," one of the young fellows called from the bow.

Clarence nodded again. "You usually find them around these mussel beds."

An 11-foot fall in the level of the water twice each day converts Narraguagus Bay into ideal worming grounds. Here, where we landed, the mud flats formed a vast expanse of bridge between two spruce forests, rising from granite ledges which were islands at high water. Clarence handed me the broken hoe and a plastic bucket.

"They can keep bloodworms in a metal pail," he said, "but sandworms will die in there. I guess the sun warms up the metal and the metal warms up the water. So we use plastic buckets, or wooden ones."

In a moment the wormers were at work, legs spread, bent from the waist, biting down into the mud and combing it away with their hoes. There were left-handed and right-handed diggers. Each man gripped his 15-inch handle in the manner of Ty Cobb wielding a bat, hands apart, the bottom one choking up a few inches, the upper one (the right, if he was right-handed) near the juncture with the metal tines. When he had rolled back a mound of mud, he removed his right hand from the handle, ran it quickly over the surface of the mud plucking off the worms, and dropped them into the bucket. (To plunge one's hand straight into the mud would be to risk having it ripped open by the jagged edges of shells and stones.) Then, without straightening up, he moved his bucket ahead and bit down again into the mud.

"Can't waste any time," Clarence said. "Out here where we find the big worms, the tide comes back in pretty fast. We only get about an hour and a half digging every tide."

I rolled back a mound of mud, but the worms were puny and hardly worth picking up. I stepped forward and dug deeper the next time, groped for a large sandworm as it wriggled off into the ooze and found myself holding only a segment of tail.

"Gotta grab quick," Clarence called. "And try to jerk 'em out by the head end. The tails break off."

I learned that one must move as well as jerk. Otherwise one becomes in fact rooted to the spot. Having stood in one place for over a minute, I had sunk into the mud nearly to my knees, and pulled myself free only with a contorted heave that left my right foot lodged somewhere above the ankle sector of its boot.

We dug on across the flats. The wormers chatted in low tones. Occasionally one broke into a fragment of song. I captured a few acceptable specimens of sandworms, as well as an eel accidentally uncovered by one of the other diggers. My arms, from fingertips to shoulders, were coated in mud that dried a light gray. Clarence straightened up, wiped his hands on his denim pants, and lit a cigarette.

"It's easier digging clams," he said. "Clams make little air holes so you can tell they're down there. Funny—all the years I was digging clams I never even noticed these worms. They must've been there. Now that I'm digging worms I never notice the clams."

"Tide's coming!" one of the others called. "Dig harder, boys!"

Each man bent over his mound of mud, trying to fill the quota he had set for himself that day. If the work appeared unnatural, the fact escaped the sandpipers and plovers that moved along unconcernedly beside me as if I were of their kind, probing the mud with a great deal less effort and, presumably, more success. Occasionally the call went up, "Tide's coming!"

I straightened up more frequently than was absolutely necessary to make notes on my mud-smeared pad. The respite could be further prolonged if I screwed my face into the expression of anxious thought expected of a literary man. Gratefully, I noticed Clarence plodding through the mud toward the boat. I joined him promptly.

"This is enough for me," he said, pointing to the worms in his bucket. "I've got maybe seven, eight hundred. Those young fellows will dig twice as many. It's a young man's trade."

I added my haul to Clarence's bucket, making, I am afraid, a very small splash. He declined the eel. The others remained at their diggings until the water began running into them. On our way back to the mainland one of the younger men nodded down at his bucket of worms, which he estimated at fifteen hundred.

"I'll count 'em out at the dealer's," he said, "and I'll get a little over forty dollars. That's pretty good for an hour and a half, plus the time to drive 'em over to the dealer's. It's hard work, all right. But it's better than working in an oil refinery."

—

Marine worms are big business in Maine. The Wall Street of wormdom is Wiscasset, a town about 150 miles west along the coast from where I live. There, worming has been carried on commercially for nearly five decades. The important dealers who set the prices are clustered around Wiscasset and they sometimes lure with more money the highly productive wormers (or buggers, as they are called in that area) from other points along the coast. It is like going to the big leagues.

But I, loyal to my neighbors, paid a visit to Addison, a Washington County town noted for its boatyards, sardine canneries, and worm dealers. The dealers are the subsidiaries of the large combines around Wiscasset and Newcastle to the west. I went to Addison mainly to see Warren Dorr, Jr., who runs the local dealership established by his father, for many years the biggest dealer in Wiscasset. Young Warren's home, a neat frame building, is not only his castle but his counting-house. In the yard stood a toy poodle, a couple of tricycles, and other indices of middle-class success. He is a stocky man in his thirties, crew-cut, horny-handed, and sparing of speech.

We descended to his cellar, a fittingly damp enclave whose darkness was relieved by a couple of unshaded electric bulbs hanging from the ceiling. Long trays covered several tables, and long, narrow cardboard boxes were stacked everywhere.

At one of the tables a man was kneading a spongy, glistening mass. On closer inspection I saw the mass was composed of hundreds of worms. The man was counting them into the cardboard boxes with all the dexterity of those ladies who used to ladle out nickels in the automat.

"When the diggers bring the worms they count them into the trays," Dorr said. "There's a screen in the bottom of the trays, and that drains the water off them."

Each wormer is beholden to a single dealer, who keeps varying numbers of them on his payroll, according to the current demand for bait. In the spring, when the weather is bad and the demand is low, a fast-working wormer may take only a thousand worms off the flats because that is all the dealer needs. Later in the season he may double that figure. Having counted the product of his day's labor into the trays, the wormer will advise the dealer of his total. Usually the man's word will be accepted, but in some cases an audit is indicated. A man caught cheating on his count may be told to peddle his worms elsewhere.

Then the worms are packed into the cardboard shipping boxes, which are lined with a cool, moist seaweed called rockweed. One box holds 125 sandworms or 250 bloodworms.

"That's because the bloodworms are much hardier," Dorr said. "The sandworms are made up of all those segments and they break up if you're not careful."

Dorr has learned from the wholesalers in New York, Florida, or California just how many worms he will have to ship out that day (they are in touch with each other regularly by telephone). Mrs. Dorr takes the boxes of worms by pickup truck to the airport at Bangor, seventy-five miles from Addison. There she supervises the loading of the worms aboard the regular flights to Boston and New York.

Dorr gets about twenty-five dollars a thousand for the sandworms, and about thirty-two dollars for the bloodworms. The city wholesalers pay the freight. In New York the wholesalers distribute the worms to the smaller bait shops, where they are sold to the fishermen. Since flounders, striped bass, and whitefish seem to relish either species, the fishermen keep calling for more.

Several fringe industries have grown up around worming. The dealers sell some of their stock to firms that trade in biological specimens. "They'll pay more," Dorr said, "but they need perfect worms and they're hard to get. Most wormers concentrate on speed and when they jerk the worms out of the mud they break off the tails."

I said I knew just what they went through. Then Dorr said that perhaps the most specialized workers in the business are the people who gather the rockweed in which the worms are packed for shipment. Some dealers employ men who do nothing but provide the rockweed, scraping it with potato hoes from rocks along the shore; they are paid twenty-five cents for a burlap bagful.

"Do bites cause the wormers much trouble?" I asked Dorr.

"Not too much," he said. "The sandworms only seem to bite when they're dried out. The bloodworms give a nasty bite, but most of the wormers have tough hands and it bothers them only when they get bit down here on the soft skin between the fingers. My mother packed worms for years and she got hard little warts on her hand where they bit her."

Worms, you might say, are almost literally in the Dorr family's blood.

"I guess so," he said. "My father was one of the first two bloodwormers in the state. He started in 1926 and then he became a dealer when the business got moving. My uncle is seventy-three years old and he still goes worming every day. He doesn't drink or smoke or even drive a car. All he does is get up in the morning and walk out on the flats and start digging."

——

What does the future hold for worms—and wormers? Testimony is contradictory. On some mud flats along the coast intensive worming apparently has depleted the supply. Yet there are other flats in Wiscasset that have been dug heavily for thirty-five years without any significant change in worm populations.

The state's Department of Sea and Shore Fisheries uses the proceeds from worming licenses to carry out studies on the worms and their habitat.

"We thought for a while we could depend on the diggers for more information about the worms," a state biologist told me. "But they don't seem to know any more than we do, which isn't very much. Take the sandworms, for instance. The wormers will find them around empty clam shells. Some of these people insist that the sandworm is the male clam."

Biologists mark the worms with silver nitrate pencils to keep track of them, just as other biologists band migratory birds. Biologists also want to know what intensive worming does to the mud flats.

"When you keep turning over the mud," the state biologist said, "you're likely to smother the clams and other small bivalves that ground-feeding fish and small crustaceans live on. Algae gets turned over, too, and it decays and forms acids in the mud."

In a recent year some 1,508,000 pounds of worms (or 65,000,000 individuals) were harvested along the Maine coast, bringing the dealers' gross sales to $1,206,923. So the state will remain the nation's bait capital for the foreseeable future. Its vast mud flats, uncovered twice a day by the considerable tides in the Gulf of Maine, provide the worms. Its economy, marked by the scarcity of other gainful employment along the coast, provides the labor. Having devastated its stands of pine, polluted its clam flats and overfished its herring, Maine now has a chance to redeem itself. If not—well, as Dorothy Parker reported after stepping on a worm:

"Aha, my little dear," I say,
"Your clan will pay me back one day!"

PART·THREE
Woods and Fields

8 ONLY GOD CAN MAKE A FOREST

I ❧   I KNOW A MAN who lives in the heart of Manhattan's filth and noise, and yet, over the years, he has identified more than one hundred species of birds in the tiny plot of trees and plants behind his brownstone house. (One of the birds was a woodcock!) The reason that the birds, chiefly migrants, come down in his East Side back yard is that in passage they have spied a green haven with its promise of food and shelter amid the concrete wasteland. This promise offered by green things fills urban yards, parks, and cemeteries with birds and other wild creatures, and helps to make the city more livable for human beings, too.

Still, few of the birds stay and manage to reproduce successfully in these small islands of green, a failure that should tell us something about the ability of such places to re-create and nourish the human spirit. As in a large greenhouse or, to make another analogy, a dying body, life is present in a technical sense but its powers to renew itself are feeble. It must be sustained from the outside.

Americans have had a curious relationship with trees ever since they invaded the forest primeval three and a half centuries ago. (There were gaps even then in that forest where the Indians had set fires to clear the land for crops or wildlife.) With the arrival of the white settlers there began an assault on the forest that, in its intensity and destructiveness, has never been equaled in the history of the world. The settlers leveled the forests to get lumber to build their homes, their ships, and a variety of wood products. They burned the forests to clear the land for towns and farms (and sometimes to deprive the wily Indians of their cover).

Maine's forests were among the first to feel the destruction, and when the loggers had taken out all the best they moved on to the Great Lakes and the South, looking for new forests to conquer. It was the waste and carelessness that appalled sensitive people during the nineteenth century. Many of the trees were left to rot where they fell; sloppy practices in the woods led to great fires, such as the one that broke out near Peshtigo, Wisconsin, in 1871, burning through two counties and killing twelve hundred people. During the worst of the destruction there were prominent men in the colleges and in government who called for the United States Army to protect the nation's woodlands.

But slowly the worst of the logging practices were brought under control, chiefly in response to the outraged protests of people who saw something noble in America's past disappearing with its forests, and partly with the agreement of the loggers themselves who finally realized that they were obliterating their own livelihood. Americans' attitudes were changing. Forests weren't always for chopping, some people began to think. The experience of many visitors to the Maine woods, from Henry Thoreau onward, was reflected in the way residents of the cities saw those woods, though they may never have been even close to Maine. Similar glowing reports of life in our vanishing forests came from all over the continent. Such terms as "multi-use" and "sustained yield" began to crop up in foresters' speech as they realized the value of opening up the forests to many kinds of experience and replanting where the trees had been logged.

Certain feelings about trees that might have seemed absurd to our ancestors began to come to the surface among sophisticated people everywhere. By going into the forest to hike or camp or canoe, or just to sit on a log and meditate, a man might retrieve a part of his humanity that his modern urban existence had smothered.

"Many times I have thought," wrote J. Frank Dobie, "that the greatest happiness to man—probably not to a woman—is to become civilized, to know the pageant of the past, to love the beautiful, to have just ideas of values and proportions, and then, retaining his animal spirits and appetites, to live in a wilderness."

For most people, women *or* men, the reality of wilderness is an extreme to be avoided, though the lure of greenery is not to be denied. I don't think that anyone who lived during the 1960s and saw the pictures of the great ghetto riots of those years on their television screens will ever forget their own conflicting feelings. Across the screen swept the panorama of violence, entire blocks burned out, chanting mobs, sweating cops, and lithe, slender-hipped figures flitting from the shadows into the garish lights and fading away again. And through one's mind swept horror, pity, frustration, and, in many cases, an overwhelming urge to go off someplace and hide. Yet the ghetto riots were simply the livid bloom on the underlying malignancy. The day-to-day procession of events was unrelieved by the pity or excitement that were the riots' residue. Crime in the streets, despair in the schools and smog that increased the incidence of urban disease were painting the forest primeval in romantic colors for those who felt trapped in a decaying civilization.

The suburbs, decked out in the eager green of spring, appeared to city-dwellers as a likely substitute for wilderness, offering the best of two worlds. A tree is a tree is a tree, one might be inclined to say, and a forest is simply a *bunch* of trees, but notions like that have let both the new suburban man and his suburban woodlands in for a lot of trouble. The fact is that many homeowners, in their ignorance of natural forces, have created a suburban ecosystem that is susceptible to catastrophe.

The homeowner is proud of his own plot of green. It is more than a status symbol, it is unquestionably a source of refreshment to a spirit troubled by an excess of civilization's artificial wares. Yet, curiously, many homeowners seem to miss the point of all this and treat their lawns and gardens precisely as another man might treat his new chrome-girdled Chrysler or Cadillac (endlessly waxing, polishing, tinkering, to maintain it in showroom splendor); both men are addicted to the hucksters' latest products and the directions to keep their prize possessions unblemished. A car may benefit from cosmetic treatments, lovingly and endlessly applied, but it is not nearly so likely that a suburban environment will.

So a man who wants his lawn to resemble a putting green deeply resents the intrusion of dandelions or crabgrass into the purity of his green domain (no matter that a stretch of green lawn flecked with the gold of dandelions delights the eye as readily as many cultivated flowers set against their garden background). He accepts the advice he reads in a gardening magazine or a seed store and douses his lawn with herbicides to extirpate the offending plants. Again, the homeowner notices a few insects nibbling on the leaves of one of his ornamental trees (no matter that in most cases this nibbling amounts only to a kind of helpful natural pruning). At the first opportunity he is out there with his chemical sprays, obliterating the nibbling insects, as well as the birds and predator insects which under natural conditions would hold the potential pests in check.

The homeowner, of course, sees no harm in all this. What possible damage could *he* cause with his insignificant pest control campaign? And, in any case, he has fallen for the chemical industry's propaganda that seems to imply that a poison is not a poison. He has read the bold type across the label of his bugbomb: NONTOXIC TO HUMANS AND PETS. But perhaps he has neglected to read the small print on the other side of the container that advises him, when using the spray, to "cover up the ornamental fish ponds," "keep away from children and pets," "don't breathe the fumes," "keep pet birds out of a room where the spray is used," and other warnings of dire consequences should the so-called nontoxic substance not be applied in the most cautious manner.

To begin with, then, this man often finds his trees and shrubs already deprived of the defense that predatory insects might have provided had they not been wiped out by him or his neighbors. In fact, many city-bred suburbanites today are disgusted and repelled by "creepy-crawlers" of any kind and so are inclined to use proportionately more chemicals on their properties than any cost-conscious farmer does. Nor do birds, or even mice, which consume large quantities of insects or their eggs and cocoons, fare much better in the average suburban environment. If they don't fall victim to its many chemical hazards, they stand little chance against the omnipresent hordes of cats and dogs.

"Detailed studies of a few species have shown that they raise very few young in suburban situations," writes Ian C. T. Nisbet of the Massachusetts Audubon Society. "It appears that suburban bird populations, especially in the inner suburbs, are maintained only by immigration from outside."

Suburban trees, deprived of these natural defenders, are open to all kinds of attacks by harmful insects which multiply in these "favorable" conditions. For a number of biological reasons, the plant-eating (or "prey") species survive chemical attacks much more easily than their predators. Because they exist in greater numbers, they have statistics on their side in the fight for survival; they breed often and in great numbers and so recover rapidly, but predators build back their populations more slowly; and, while the sprays do not often reach all of the pests, their predators search out and consume the victims, thus building up the poisons in their own bodies and falling victim in their turn.

Even in the absence of a chemical barrage the homeowner is likely to discover that his trees probably are suffering from an overdose of modern civilization. Poisoned by the leaded fumes of passing autos, parched by drainage patterns that have been altered by drains and sewers, encased in concrete and strangled by a maze of underground pipes and wires, the suburban tree is fair game for troublesome insects and diseases. Despite what its owners believe is loving care, that tree and those around it are all too often simply a part of the unhealthy suburban woodlands. Blight, often nourished by modern ways of life, reaches into the suburbs, and beyond.

II 𖧷   AND WHAT HAS all this to do with the Maine woods? It seems a very long step indeed from a back yard and what is left of its surrounding woodlands in a Chicago or a Memphis suburb to the Maine woods, but a durable bridge links them. Each area is an ecosystem, and what links them in their present troubles is man's ecological ignorance. This deficiency is nothing new. But when it is accompanied by the technological marvels that man recently has devised in his ingenuity and turned loose on the American landscape in his ignorance, the results alter both our lives and our various environments.

That both types of woodland are vastly changed from what they were two hundred years ago goes without saying. Even the North American forests of pre-Columbian times changed repeatedly for a number of reasons, including climatic alterations and natural disasters such as lightning-ignited fires—indeed 155 of the 300 forest fires reported in Maine during a recent year were touched off by lightning. But man has accelerated the pace of change. In heavily settled areas the forests came under all kinds of pressure, as man cut the trees and often started damaging forest fires. Three-quarters of the forests in Massachusetts and Rhode Island have been burned at least once in the last century. These fires tended to destroy the woodland's diversity, favoring the thick-barked, fire-resistant oaks, which are almost completely dominant today in some areas. Like the great agricultural fields planted to a single crop, such woodlands are especially susceptible to insect and disease. (Oaks, for instance, are among the favorite trees of the gypsy moth, which has become a major pest in several of the eastern states.)

In Maine, the coveted white pines were scattered in clumps and veins among other trees of the northern forests, particularly the spruces, which the loggers looked upon as "weed trees." The clumps of great pines were taken. But Maine's forests were not decimated as they were in many other parts of the country because the spruce, which made up the forests' bulk, were often spared.

The timbermen gained control over so much of Maine's interior during the nineteenth century because its thin, rocky soil was not suited to farming. That most of Maine's land fell into the hands of a small body of men who represented one rather rapacious industry no doubt retarded the state's general development. Traditionally, the timber interests have controlled the state legislature. Today the ten largest paper companies own about one-third of the state's land and pay taxes of less than thirty-five cents an acre. Great rivers, such as the Kennebec, as well as the forests, fell under the industry's control in the nineteenth century. The rivers were taken over to float logs to the company mills. (Dams and locks actually turned around a part of the flow in the Allagash basin so that the logs could be floated to the Penobscot River rather than the St. John, which runs for much of its length through Canada.) Later on, wastes from the pulp mills destroyed the fish and other resources on those rivers.

Today still another conglomerate seems to have entered the picture. ITT (International Telephone and Telegraph) has infiltrated Maine as mysteriously, if not as actively, as it has Chile, provoking all sorts of speculation. Through a sub-subsidiary, ITT recently invested three million dollars in about seventy thousand acres of land (twenty thousand acres of which the company acquired on leases) in northwestern Maine. Rumors about ITT's eventual plans for the land mention a variety of projects ranging from housing developments, four-season resorts, and a wood-products industry all the way to turning it over to the United States Navy to construct a huge underground communications system.

In a very real sense, ITT's less sophisticated predecessors, the pioneer timbermen, contributed to the preservation of the state's extensive wildlands. They discouraged settlement in the vast areas they owned or otherwise controlled, fearing that settlers would start untamable forest fires and, should profitable settlements arise in the timberlands, that taxes would go up for all the landowners alike. It is to these unsettled areas that hunters, fishermen, campers, and canoeists flock from all over the East today for recreation. Moreover, by cutting openings in the impenetrable forest ("Letting the sun into the swamp," as the old-timers said), the loggers provided a more suitable and diversified habitat for deer and other wildlife.

After the tall white pines disappeared, the timbermen turned to the spruces and found, to their surprise and profit, that they, too, yielded good boards. Although individual spruces do not provide the amount of wood that a giant pine did, they easily reproduce themselves and grow to maturity much more quickly. Technology itself produced important changes later on. While the use of wood for many products declined when other materials became available, wood pulp replaced linen and other fibers as the chief ingredient in paper. (Like many other changes, this has not been all to the good; librarians report that books made of wood pulp do not last nearly as long as those made from the traditional fibers, and the shelves in libraries now are full of books whose paper is yellowing and cracking so that they fall apart as soon as they are touched.)

The pulp mills revolutionized forestry itself. The mills, expensive to build and equip, could not be moved as the old sawmills had been when the supply of nearby timber ran out. Because trees must be maintained within a reasonable distance of the pulp mills, the paper companies themselves resorted to tree-planting and other conservation practices. Lumber production in this country has declined since World War II, but wood pulp production has risen 313 per cent. And, despite their operators' protestations to the contrary, pulp mills remain notorious polluters of the air and water around them.

In some of Maine's company towns the local people will put up with "the smell of money," enduring the contaminated air that peels the paint from their houses and destroys their lungs, in return for the jobs the company provides. But when their practices affect outside lives the companies begin to come under various pressures, especially from sportsmen, government agencies, and those conservationists and recreationists who make up "the boondock lobby." Sport fishermen want to see the pulp mills' chemical effluents curtailed so that the Atlantic salmon and other game fish can be restored in the rivers. The traditional log drives on the rivers are coming to an end, killed in large part by the complaints of recreationists and the owners of riparian rights who objected to the paper companies' inclination to take over entire rivers for this purpose. And now, for the sportsmen, the paper companies' forestry techniques are coming full circle: where the loggers once opened up the forests to provide better forage for the deer herds, the powerful new machines that "clear-cut" whole forests are destroying those areas for wildlife.

"We do not have good woodland habitat now," a state game biologist recently told the *Maine Sunday Telegram*.

Before bulldozers and especially before skidders, a logging operation would cover between ten and 500 acres annually.

Now it starts at 500 and goes into the thousands. There used to be many more nut trees in the woods. Many beech and oak were not of the quality necessary for logs. They were left standing and provided food for deer of much higher quality than winter browse and which was available immediately before and after the hard winter yarding months. This food is no longer there. Modern logging for pulp and logs creates huge openings in the forest canopy.

At the root of the trouble is the fact that the men who make their living from the forests are often as naïve or as indifferent as the new homeowner on his small suburban lot. They fail to see that the landscape is not simply a bunch of trees but rather a complex community of plants and animals dependent on the soil and water around them. In the interests of "efficiency," the homeowner pours chemicals in profusion on a variety of plants (some of which are not even suited to that area) so that he can save time and labor while impressing his neighbors with the results. The large woodland owners want to take out wood as quickly and as cheaply as possible. In both cases the living community is sacrificed to short-term efficiency.

Spruce grows rapidly, and thus the forests are cut over often, perhaps every fifty years or so, while the longer-lived trees like pine, that would have added diversity to the forest, are given no chance to mature. (It takes three hundred years or more for a white pine *forest* to reach maturity, though individual trees may be harvested earlier.) According to Neil Jorgensen, the biologist who wrote *A Guide to New England's Landscape*, "Forest investigators doubt that devastating outbreaks of disease and insect attacks similar to those of modern times occurred over widespread areas of the primeval forest. Smaller outbreaks may have occurred, however, following damage by fire or wind."

A healthy forest community—i.e., a diversified one—was able to withstand insect outbreaks far better than today's much-abused woodlands. Because foresters did not understand the complexities of this community, they attempted to "eradicate" pest insects after World War II with massive aerial doses of the new wonder chemical, DDT. The result, in most places, has been disastrous. Insect parasites and predators which had kept the defoliating insects in a reasonable balance with the surrounding forest community were wiped out, letting the pests escape control. It was during the heyday of DDT, for instance, that the gypsy moth threw off its natural shackles in southern New England to begin the alarming extension of its range that we observe today.

Was this simply a coincidence? In 1971 a meeting was held at the United States Department of Agriculture's Administration Building in Washington, D.C., to discuss alternate methods (such as biological controls) of dealing with the gypsy moth. The experts finally had realized that their exclusive reliance on the aerial spraying of insecticides had failed. During the meeting, Reitz I. Sailer, who has studied the gypsy moth with USDA's Agricultural Research Service for many years, spoke of that insect's "suddenly violent fluctuations" during the 1950s.

"I can't help but feel that we were seeing evidence of human interference with the natural balance that had stabilized the gypsy moth's population in the 1930s," Sailer said. "If you spray over a large area you annihilate all the parasites. We went from a policy of coexistence to one of annihilation, and we have not been successful. That's why we're here today."

In northern Maine conservationists finally forced the Maine Forest Service to abandon its endless spraying with DDT over large areas of the forest to control the spruce budworm. The forest had lived with its insects for untold centuries until man interfered on a massive scale. Today those forests are "hooked" on pesticides, just as an addict is hooked on his favorite drug. We have created a whole new set of problems for ourselves. Until we find a way out, the birds, fish, and other members of the complex forest community will suffer more than the "pests" that we, to a large extent, brought into being with our bungled manipulations.

America's changing values, then, are altering its economic calculations. In the dispute over the supersonic transport plane (SST), these values influenced the decision to scrap the plane because of its potential impact on the environment. Congress abandoned the SST-construction program although its decision meant that jobs and contracts would be lost in the Seattle area, where economic difficulties already abounded. In this case America struck a blow against the foolish notion that we must solve our economic problems by putting people to work destroying the environment. At the other end of the continent these new public attitudes have posed a challenge to Maine's paper companies.

Consider the plight of the Scott Paper Company, which owns a pulp mill in Winslow. The mill was built in 1891 and has polluted the broad Kennebec River ever since. In recent years, however, the company has come under pressure from government agencies and the public to clean up its pulp wastes, though the cost of installing a waste-treatment plant in this aging mill would reach at least thirty million dollars. Scott is faced with adding the treatment plant to a mill that may soon be obsolete in any case, or building a modern mill with a treatment plant included. But other factors intrude. The dilemma comes for Scott at a time when events elsewhere in the world have cut into its sales. These developments have been listed by the *Maine Times:*

Competition for its consumer products (paper towels, toilet and facial tissue) was intense, and marketing efforts by wealthy competitors like Lever Brothers cut into Scott's sales—so much so that production estimates at Winslow had to be curtailed. At the same time, demand for the other leading Winslow products—paper stock for data cards—was cut nearly in half as the war in Vietnam "wound down" and military computers slowed; the same was true for the aerospace industry computers, the other large consumer of the Scott product. As a result of the public yearning for peace, the vote against the SST and a general moderation of intense computer technology, Scott planners saw their cash reserves vanish.

Obviously a third choice confronts Scott, as it does other Maine paper companies with similar troubles. It may find that its best interests lie in shutting down the mill permanently, a solution that would throw a thousand millworkers and perhaps five hundred woodcutters out of work. And, indeed, the paper companies are taking steps to phase out their traditional business of harvesting the trees and grinding them into paper products. In this they are taking advantage of their position as Maine's largest landholders. Their economists have discovered that the companies earn only about a dollar a year for each acre they keep in the production of forest trees, but if they used the best land for recreational developments (lakeside camps, ski installations, camp grounds, etc.) they would earn at least eight dollars an acre. It is a tempting possibility, but one which does not enthuse the men who have earned their living by cutting the trees or working in the mills.

III 🌿 A CURIOUS MANPOWER PROBLEM has already cropped up in connection with Maine's forests. In settled areas along the coast there are dwindling opportunities for work.

"There's not much real work in the woods around here any more," says an old-timer who lives in a coastal town. "You've got a few guys going in there now all year round with tractors and chain saws. They take the place of God knows how many people who used to work in the woods during the winter. They'd spend the winter in there, when it was easier to get out the logs on the ice and snow than at any other time of year, and there were no black flies and mosquitoes. They'd chop down trees, and drive logs in the spring, and then come out and if they had a farm they were ready to start working on it."

Yet in the vast forested interior the big landowners have the same sort of problem that the owners of fishing boats have: the work is hard and the pay (though two hundred dollars a week or more) is no longer enough to entice strong-backed men to leave their families for long periods and do the job that has to be done. Only some French-Canadian laborers are willing to do this work, and the owners must depend upon them to get the logs out of the Maine woods.

"The Americans will drive a truck for you," a woods boss says. "My drivers are Americans. But they won't cut wood, so I hire Canadians who will."

To fill in the ranks in their labor force the woodland owners have gone pretty far afield: someone's bright idea that Southern blacks could handle the job flickered out when the weather turned cold and the blacks retreated to sunnier lands. In one area the owners have had better success with Tibetan refugees who followed the Dalai Lama to this country and found the spartan conditions in the Maine woods to their liking.

Along the coast today the woodland harvest is mainly seasonal. The state was a pioneer in the production of Christmas trees, most of them balsam firs which tend to hold their needles longer after the tree has been cut than do other evergreens. But, like so much else in the state, the Christmas-tree business is declining. In 1950 the growers shipped one million trees to dealers in other states. The figure fell to three hundred thousand trees in 1968, and by 1971 the growers shipped out less than one hundred thousand.

"In my mind, the reason for the drop is that for many years Maine shipped relatively low-quality trees in vast numbers," said Lewis P. Bissell, a forester who is secretary of the Maine Christmas Tree Growers Association. "You don't have to be a prophet to know that when low-quality trees are marketed, people will turn to supplies of very high-quality trees from plantations near the cities."

One of the few opportunities the people of eastern Maine still have to make a profit with their forest products is in an area where individual skill and patience count heavily. Canada and eastern Maine, with their reservoirs of cheap labor, send a steady flow of Christmas wreaths to the big cities during the holidays. In our community the weaving of wreaths by hand is a flourishing, if evanescent, enterprise.

The entrepreneurs in this line are generally "people from away," either buying the wreaths directly from the residents who make them in their homes or setting up temporary factories where the wreaths are fashioned and packed for shipment to the cities. The necessary prelude to wreath-making is called variously "tipping" or "brushing," when whole families fan out through the woods collecting evergreen twigs and branches. Anyone's land is fair game. Occasionally a landowner becomes miffed when a tipper cuts down his balsam firs to get at the upper branches, but in general the practice is tolerated just as people tolerate the hunters who tramp across their land during the deer season.

The art of fashioning wreaths from these evergreen tips is devilishly tough on a person's hands. In Maine, this is usually a woman's job. A few hours at this sort of work converts the hands you love to touch into a pair of scratched-up, pitch-stained grappling hooks that might embarrass a grease monkey, but the women cheerfully put up with the occupational hazards in return for additional cash at the holiday season. Many of them earn up to twenty-five dollars a day at the wreath factory. The women whose job it is to trim the wreaths with pine cones and holly berries find the sharp wire fastenings much more annoying, and so before going into the factories they bind their hands with tape as meticulously as a prize fighter who is about to enter the ring.

One day when I was talking to my friend Clifford West, a

lobster fisherman, and his wife, Ann, the talk came around to Christmas wreaths. Clifford groaned.

"'Clifford *hates* me to make wreaths." Ann laughed. She is in her late twenties, with a cheerful round face and a pleasantly husky voice.

"Have you ever been in a house where they made wreaths?" Clifford asked. "Why, you can go in there a year later and still make wreaths!"

"It is pretty messy," Ann agreed ruefully. "You wonder how the sprills even get upstairs, but you find them in your bed and all over."

"After we get our house fixed up, that's when I draw the line," Clifford said. "Yessir!"

"We always made them when we were kids," Ann said. "The little kids would go brushing, and the older ones would make the wreaths. My mother did pretty good at it."

"Oh, you can do good at it," Clifford said. "I know a fellow in Steuben who's even better than his wife at making wreaths, and they earn about three thousand dollars during the season."

"Sure," Ann nodded. "I made them up until a couple of years ago—just to get money to buy Clifford a Christmas present—and I'd get sixty cents for a fourteen-inch wreath. I liked to collect the brush, but, to tell you the truth, I never cared much for making wreaths."

There is no longer a place for the iron men who felled the giant pines with their axes. The world has changed, and so has its needs. The Maine woods, which once provided masts for a king's ships, now produce paper napkins, Christmas wreaths, and water pollution.

9

WAY DOWN
ON THE FARM

SOME YEARS AGO I was in Washington, D.C., completing research for a book I was writing about water pollution. On my rounds I spoke to a number of legislative assistants and other Congressional aides. One of them steered me toward another story.

"You know," he said, "when you finish your book you ought to write a magazine article about the revolution in food marketing. The President's appointed a commission to look into the whole thing. They've come up with some pretty good stuff."

I had my name put on the commission's mailing list, and over the next few months a flood of material reached me in Maine. My informant had been right, for this material added up to a good story. The way we get our food is of special concern to anyone like myself who is interested in the natural world. One doesn't have to be a faddist to realize that attractive and tasty foods are produced in a healthy environment, while misguided attempts to push the land beyond its productive capacity have poisoned that environment in a number of ways. President Lyndon B. Johnson's Commission on Food Marketing made plain the nature of this revolution: while standardizing (and sometimes improving) America's food supply, it has altered our eating habits, dislocated rural lives, and contributed substantially to America's pollution problems.

I made some attempts to interest magazine editors in the material, but without success. Publications such as the *New Republic* asked their regulars to cover the story, but the average general-circulation magazine, which is dependent on food advertising, wasn't very enthusiastic about the commission's critical remarks on the system. Meanwhile, as the material poured in, Ada (who was teaching the fifth and sixth grades in nearby Sullivan at the time) read through a good part of it. She believed that the commission's material, if properly extracted and digested from the mass of summaries, charts, graphs, and tables, was ideally suited to explain an American phenomenon to children.

"You can write a lot of complicated and controversial things for children that a woman's magazine wouldn't touch," she said, and then added, bristling, "If the women's magazines are any indication, American women are absolutely *mindless*. And the editors of women's magazines seem determined to keep them that way."

She was right, of course, and we set to work on a book for "young readers" which we called *The Great American Shopping Cart*. I don't know whether it has helped children understand this part of the American way, but in the process of writing the book some things became clearer to me.

For one thing, it supported with facts the complaints of the grower that he, the single most important man in the entire assembly line that puts food on our table, is also at the bottom of the economic ladder.

In many cases the grower receives no more for his product, whether it is wheat or potatoes, than he did thirty or forty years ago. He stays alive only by assembling larger farms to produce his crop in bulk and by the sometimes self-defeating practice of loading up his fields with pesticides and fertilizers to extract the highest possible yield per acre. (If his pesticides wipe out insect parasites and predators, he must keep increasing the amounts of these "commercial poisons," thus increasing his operating costs; if they wipe out pollinating insects, he creates other problems for himself, as we shall see.)

In any event, there is usually a considerable gap between the price the grower receives for his crop, and the price the consumer pays for it at the other end of the line. Part of the money goes to brokers, wholesalers, and shippers. Other parts of the final cost go for such significant items as gasoline and the highway tolls required to transport the produce in refrigerated trucks, newspaper advertisements placed by the supermarket chain, plastic rolls in which to wrap the produce, shopping carts in which to roll the purchased groceries through the store—and, let us hope, a new waste-treatment system at the processing plant.

Where Americans once ate the bulk of their fruits and vegetables fresh, today they eat them more often out of a can or a frozen pack. And thus the gap between the price paid at the farm and at the supermarket widens further. A grower sells a load of peas for $24. But the buyer, who plans to can the peas, must pay $26 for the cans to put them in, $2.25 for alluring labels to paste on his cans, and another $2.50 for the cartons in which to ship the finished product.

A consumer who buys whole potatoes and prepares them "hash-browned" for her family spends about four cents for each serving. The same consumer, who prefers the built-in "maid service" provided by processed hash-browned potatoes, finds that they cost her nearly twice as much for a serving.

The revolution in technology and marketing has altered American tastes, too, so that the consumer believes processed foods to be worth the price. In 1947, 683 million pounds of American fruits and vegetables were sold as frozen foods.

Twenty years later that figure rose to more than 4 *billion* pounds. Today one out of every four dollars spent in American grocery stores buys the "convenience" foods that are products of the huge dry-grocery manufacturing business. These products range from prepared frozen dinners, canned fish, breakfast cereals, and instant potatoes to packaged desserts, pet foods, and dehydrated soup mixes.

Maine, with its short growing season, poor soil, and its transportation problems, is not endowed to compete with the regions that have contributed to the food-marketing revolution. Its crops, then, are usually the ones fitted for the region by nature and traditionally grown by the local people. Thus life styles have been slow to change. It came as something of a shock to everybody several years ago when the chairman of the state's Environmental Improvement Commission revealed that several national food processors finally had rejected opportunities to establish plants in Maine when they learned that the water supply in this water-rich state was insufficient; the labor they needed was located only near rivers that had been polluted so badly by the pulp mills that the water was unfit for these firms' specialized requirements.

The state's largest agricultural business remains poultry. Raising broilers is big business, and the landscape is dotted with those dreary sheet-metal factories where honest chicks are converted by the miracle of modern care and feeding not into toothsome birds but into pounds of bland blubber. It is precisely these aspects of factory farming that enable Maine chicken growers and processors to remain in business. Were it not for the most "progressive" methods, the Maine poultry industry would be unable to bear the high cost of importing feed grains from the Midwest. (Maine chicken farmers pay four dollars a ton more for this grain than their counterparts in the Southeast because of the antiquated railroad system in the state.) Still, poultry business, like much else that is profitable in Maine, is generally confined to the southern counties; the broiler processors, where they managed to set up shop around

Belfast in eastern Maine, proved to be gross polluters of Penobscot Bay.

The crops on which northeastern Maine depends are blueberries and potatoes. The region is remote from the rest of the United States, its population is steadily declining, and yet its troubles are closely tied to what has gone wrong in the nation as a whole. I think that nothing illustrates this final complication more fittingly than the bear hunters of the blueberry barrens.

Every summer I take a breeding-bird census for the United States Fish and Wildlife Service in this area, and part of my route takes me through the blueberry barrens. The barrens stretch for some miles on sandy, well-drained soils just inland from the coast in Washington County. It is a landscape of general flatness, scooped out here and there at the site of present or vanished lakes, and covered by low woody plants, most of which are low-bush blueberries. The berries grow wild over much of this part of the country. Here, in the commercial fields on the barrens, they are encouraged in a variety of ways. The large owners irrigate their land with water from the many ponds and streams, kill competing plants by mowing and spraying, and burn the fields regularly. ("Nobody knows exactly what good this burning does—that's just one of the mysteries connected with blueberries—but it does seem to help them grow better berries," a botanist has told me. "I suppose it's a combination of things, pruning back the roots, so to speak, and strengthening them, and adding ashes to the soil, which fertilizes them. And then, of course, burning over the ground helps to kill the insects.") Finally, the landowners send crop-dusters over the fields several times each summer. DDT was once heavily used on the blueberry barrens, but it has been phased out in recent years. Today dieldrin, a close relative of DDT, is still commonly used to kill thrips, while such nonpersistent insecticides as Guthion are applied to kill maggots.

Often in early summer, as I drive along one of the narrow

bumpy dirt roads that lace the barrens, I see clouds of bees swarming over the delicate little pink-and-white blueberry flowers, and in the distance their hives stacked in the fields. And a little later on I invariably pass a pickup truck, its driver and a rifle-toting partner surveying the countryside. The two sights are more closely connected than the casual observer might suppose. Like so many crops, blueberries are pollinated by insects, chiefly bees. But the insecticides used by the growers make no distinctions, blotting out insect friends and foes alike. The bees native to the area have long since been poisoned, so the growers are obliged to hire bees from professional beekeepers at ten dollars a hive to pollinate their berries. The beekeepers stack the hives in the fields, where very often they are raided for their honey by bears from the nearby thickets. And so, as in some fairy story, the pickup trucks patrol the roads to kill the bears that raid the hives of rented bees that replace the native bees that have been killed by insecticides. Ah, Lewis Carroll, thou shouldst be living at this hour!

When the berries ripen in August the barrens are invaded by an army of men, women, and children (many of whom are Indians, imported from Canada for the purpose) who harvest the berries. The rocky, uneven nature of the barren's terrain discourages the use of mechanical harvesters, so the berries are gathered with wide, toothed scoops called "rakes." The berries are taken from the barrens on trucks to the "factories." There they are cleaned and dumped on rolling belts. Alongside the belts sit women who "pick them over" for twigs, leaves, and other foreign matter as they roll past.

Though these pulpy little fruits are probably the tastiest blueberries in the world (far surpassing the large "high-bush" blueberry), the growers make little effort to market them fresh. Instead the berries are put in cans at the local factories to be sold with various muffin and cake mixes. Nevertheless, there is some concern that the local blueberry industry may lose out to more mechanized operations in other parts of the country;

efficiency, rather than tastiness, seems to rule the food industry, as anyone who buys supermarket bread, tomatoes, cookies, and chickens is aware.

The women in our community like the money they make at the factories during the brief packing season, but few families pile into trucks and cars and head for the barrens to pick berries as they once did. That is increasingly considered to be work fit only for Indians. How long will this labor supply last? No one knows, but growers in other parts of the country who are dependent on labor to hand-pick their fruit crops know that they cannot plant any more fruit than they are absolutely sure they have pickers for.

"Some of these people are very stubborn," said Radcliff Pike, Sumner's brother and a botanist for many years at the University of New Hampshire. "They've claimed for a long time that blueberries can't be cultivated—that you just have to let them grow wild. But I know that you can grow them from seed. They should be experimenting, raising *selected* strains from seed or cuttings, and planting and harvesting them mechanically. With the terrific competition they're getting now from the growers of high-bush blueberries, they're going to wake up one day in Washington County and find they've lost the blueberry market."

Who are "they"? Well, in most cases the local factories are owned by men or by families with strong ties to the community. Hollis Wyman, for instance, owns one of the sardine canneries and one of the blueberry canneries. His family can be traced back to the very beginnings of our town and, indeed, a section of the town bears his family name. A conservative Republican in the old Maine tradition, he is one of the party's leaders in the state Senate. He operates in the manner of an old-fashioned city politician, distributing largesse to the poor at Christmas, making sure old folks are delivered to the polls on Election Day, and keeping an eye on local matters in general. Like most of the other big businessmen here, his ownership extends not only to the canneries and machinery themselves, but also to the boats, trucks, and even the thousands of acres of land on which the berries grow.

There is some disgruntlement about the way these men manage things, of course, though no one is likely to shout it from the roof tops. A complaint among some local workers is that the cannery owners discourage well-paying, year-round industries from entering the area, thus keeping a large pool of hungry workers available to staff the canneries in season. This part of Maine undoubtedly fulfills the conditions that industrialists in every country have always cherished: "Water plentiful and labor docile." As we shall see, there are other reasons beyond provincial skullduggery for keeping most industries out of Washington County, but I had an experience one day with Senator Wyman that I thought suggestive. It was at the time that oil had first been mentioned as a solution to the county's economic problems. The phone rang, and I recognized Wyman's high-pitched voice.

"Say, I've got a couple of newspapermen in my office from Portland," he said. "Would you like to come down and talk to them about oil?"

It was the first time I had been asked to come to Wyman's office. "Sure," I said, "I'll go anywhere to talk about oil."

Wyman's office is in a small frame building at the edge of the town's business section. A slender man, gray of face and hair, he was sitting behind a desk in his comfortable, roomy office. The newspapermen were putting questions to him about the blessings and problems oil might bring to the county. At each question, Wyman deferred to me.

"What do *you* think about that?" he'd ask me.

When I had given my answer, Wyman invariably turned to the newspapermen and nodded enthusiastically.

"Now that's a very interesting answer," he would say. "I never thought of it like that. Of course, I've really been too busy to give the whole thing much thought. But that's an interesting answer, don't you think?"

Not being versed in political maneuver, I didn't understand

at first what was taking place. It was only after I'd answered most of Wyman's questions for him that it occurred to me why he had asked me to sit in on the interview. He knew of my opposition to oil facilities in the county. I was stating for the press the case against the entry of a new industry, while the Senator did not have to be quoted on a position that might be offensive to some of his constituents. Far from being indignant, however, I was happy to see those views publicized. The Senator and I, it could be said, had entered into a symbiotic relationship.

—

McDonald's, a nation-wide chain of "fast-food stores," boasts in its advertising about the billions of hamburgers it has already sold in its brief history. It sells enormous quantities of French-fried potatoes, too—including two thousand pounds a week through its outlet in the heart of Maine's potato country—but not a single one of those potatoes was grown in Maine. This somewhat humiliating revelation prompted the executive vice-president of the Maine Potato Council to write an aggrieved letter to the chairman of the board at McDonald's. But otherwise the local response was one of amused surprise rather than of indignation. "Maineacs" become inured to disappointment.

"Surely this should be a spur to Maine spud growers and distributors," the *Bangor Daily News* commented in an editorial. "And so should the criticisms that have come from housewives and restaurant operators who make complaints about sizing, washing and inconsistency of quality."

The *News* hoped that Maine's potato industry, which once led the nation, would do better in the future. But matters seem to have passed out of the potato farmer's hands. Like so many of their fellows in eastern Maine, they are fighting both the national revolution in marketing and technology and the troubles that are peculiar to their region.

For Maine, crippling national competition is already a reality. Aroostook County, north of us here in Washington

County and larger than Delaware and Rhode Island combined, is potato country. There, in summer, the potato fields stretch away in a blur of white blossoms to the far horizon. At one time Aroostook potatoes provided ninety per cent of the starch used in American industry, and nourished millions of American families.

Aroostook farmers no longer enjoy this favored position. Today industry gets its starch from a variety of products, including corn. Idaho and other Western states, often equipped with vast federally constructed irrigation projects which Maine does not have, grow potatoes that claim a large share of the market. Overproduction helps to keep prices down, so that Maine growers receive barely more for their crop than they did forty years ago. Prices, in fact, fluctuate wildly for potatoes ($2.32 per hundredweight in 1959, $1.14 in 1961, and $3.82 in 1964), but today the Maine farmer seldom receives the $2.40 it costs him to grow a hundredweight.

Nor are there any federal price supports for potatoes, as there are for many other crops. Federal subsidies that were in effect for potatoes during World War II were dropped partly because Maine potato farmers, disdaining "government handouts," showed little enthusiasm for them. The potato farmers always relished their reputation as "gamblers." One year they were in trouble, the next they were driving Cadillacs.

Now the potato business seems to be chronically depressed. In the face of severe competition from the Western states, the potato farmers find it particularly galling that the producers of different kinds of foods disparage potatoes in their promotion and advertising. The notion that potatoes are fattening has gained considerable ground nationally in recent years, badly hurting the potato farmers. The rice industry has been a special villain in this respect, telling the diet-conscious public that rice makes a fine substitute for high-caloric foods such as potatoes. The potato farmers complained to the Federal Trade Commission, pointing out that potatoes, in fact, are low in calories; half a cup of boiled potatoes contains only 45 calories, the same amount of rice contains 100 calories, and a baked potato has only 90. But the public drenches its potatoes in butter or sour cream and goes on complaining that "potatoes are fattening." And the potato farmers starve.

One by one, these people, who want nothing better from life than to be able to grow potatoes, are being forced to sell their land. In the last twenty years the number of potato farms in Aroostook County has dropped from 4600 to 1300. Where do all these people go when they have abandoned their farms? Many of them leave the county or even the state for new opportunities. The county's population dropped from 106,000 in 1960 to 94,000 in 1970; but when the statisticians mix in the natural increase attributed to more births than deaths they estimate that one out of every four residents left the county during that period. Those who remain must struggle for a living. More than twenty per cent of Aroostook people receive surplus food from the federal government. Grumbling is occasionally heard that jobs are going begging in the woods while residents line up for surplus food and unemployment compensation. This complaint is better left unstated. Cutting pulpwood in the northern forest is dangerous and backbreaking work even with modern machinery, and if it does not always require a Paul Bunyan, it wants something more than a part-time ribbon clerk. Woodcutting chews men up, and many of them are no longer fit for it when they reach their fifties.

Some of the farmers stay in business, so to speak, by selling their land to the processors and raising potatoes for them on salary. Increasingly, it seems to make little difference. More of the potatoes are going to the plant, in any case. Although the volume of potatoes consumed is the largest in the fresh-vegetable field, the proportion is sinking, so that today about one-half of all Maine potatoes are shipped to processing plants.

And modern life is further disrupted. Potato processing, like so much of the new technology, pollutes its surroundings and, in one instance at least, led to some bizarre and far-reaching consequences.

10 THAT MESS ON THE PRESTILE

I ❧ WHEN WE LEFT eastern Maine on Route 6 we encountered a curious monument beside the road only fifty feet inside the Canadian border. It was a large concrete slab, ten feet tall and tapering toward its flat, unadorned top. A plaque on its face bore this scrap of local history, recorded in words which suggested not so much the celebration of some dimly remembered event but rustic defiance in the face of a still menacing aggressor:

THIS INTERNATIONAL MONUMENT
Symbolizes the beginning of the Citizens' War on Pollution in Western New Brunswick and Eastern Maine, and marks the site where aroused citizens built an earthen dam to stem the flow of pollution from the Vahlsing Inc. complex in Easton, Maine
9 July 1968
This date marked the beginning of
our War on Pollution
The War Continues

We had to look closely to detect the remains of the storied dam. The ground sloped sharply down from the road through alder thickets to a stream whose width and well-being varied with the season. This was the Prestile Stream, puny even at its most robust compared with its notoriety, like those rivers raised to the divine in mythology but which remind disillusioned tourists in modern Greece only of the little creek back home. On the far side of the stream some earth had been gouged out of the bank. Limbs of a few small fallen trees pierced the water's moving surface. This was all that remained of a dam whose existence was as brief as that of any May fly which annually appears and mates over the stream.

I was in New Brunswick on an assignment, from *American Heritage*, to write an article about that international incident conservationists had been calling "the mess on the Prestile." The stream rises near Fort Fairfield in northern Maine, flows south and east for twenty-five miles through the Aroostook County towns of Easton, Mars Hill, Blaine, and Bridgewater, and enters New Brunswick at Centreville. From Centreville it winds another ten miles through a pleasant valley to Florenceville, where it contributes its waters (and apparently a great deal else besides) to the St. John River. Shortly before Ada and I arrived on its banks, the Prestile had concluded an eventful decade by falling nomenclaturally into Canadian hands. Authorities on both sides of the border had put an end to age-old confusion by accepting the Canadian name— Presque Isle—for the stream's entire length. And so, like Palestine and Indo-China, the Prestile enters history as the obsolete name of a contemporary battleground.

We drove along the Prestile (for so it shall ever be to conservationists) until we found its junction with the St. John. Once there, we decided to walk along the stream for a while. When we had scrambled down an embankment from the road, we found rocks along the shore were coated with a slimy, gray substance which we needed no chemist to analyze for us. If one has ever smelled a truly rotten potato, then only a little imagination is needed to guess what the smell of the remains of *thousands* of rotten potatoes must be. Ada gagged and retreated to the car. I stuck it out for a few minutes in the interests of science, then joined her, and we drove back to Centreville to talk to Bob Caines.

Caines, who once was Centreville's mayor, is chiefly responsible for both the dam and its monument. Of middle age and placid disposition, he is an unlikely crusader. In fact, he had been an electrician for many years, but Centreville is a town of fewer than five hundred people, and correspondingly few walls to be rewired and toasters to be repaired. Caines finally followed the path taken by most of Centreville's wage earners and went to work for a large food-processing plant on the St. John River. His choice of jobs was dictated by an idealism not often found in a middle-aged man who has dabbled in politics; anxious to learn more about the subject to which he was originally drawn in anger, Caines went to work operating the food company's waste-treatment plant.

"We're going to prove that industries don't have to go on polluting the rivers," Caines told me. "We've had some problems getting started here. We've gone at it on a trial-and-error basis and we've had to modify the equipment when we found its weak spots. But I know now that any industry can clean up its wastes if it wants to."

The story that Caines told me of the mess on the Prestile had its origins far from Centreville. It was the inevitable issue of that enduring love affair carried on in Maine between politicians and the leaders of industry; and even so prominent a pollution fighter as Senator Edmund S. Muskie found to his embarrassment that in this case he had been lumped with the polluters. In its restricted flow the pretty little Prestile carried as neat a morality tale as the greatest rivers on the continent.

The stream is both pretty and productive when not overburdened with pollution. In 1955 a report of the Maine Department of Inland Fish and Game described the Prestile's cool shallow flow and the fish it supported:

Prestile Stream has been famous for its brook trout fishing for many years. . . . Trout of all sizes abound in most of the tributary streams, reflecting the excellent quality of the spawning nursery and resident areas for this species.

For many people sport or beauty is implicit in the concept of flowing water. But to others it suggests nothing more than it did to the emergent barbarians in medieval cities, who flung household wastes into the rainwater that ran through their narrow streets. Maine's industrialists seem to share this inclination. The state's major industries—pulp mills, potato-processing plants, tanneries, and woolen mills—have always been gross polluters of its waterways. But the big companies were not solely responsible for the early steps in the Prestile's degradation. The local people, acting individually or as the citizenry of various towns, contributed their share of pollution; farmers dumped the potatoes they couldn't sell along the stream's banks, towns like Mars Hill dumped into its flow their untreated sewage.

But the state prodded Mars Hill to install a sewage-treatment plant. Some farmers mended their erring ways. Attention began to shift to Vahlsing, Incorporated, which opened a potato-processing plant on the Prestile in 1960. Though its main office is in Robbinsville, New Jersey, the company operates food-processing plants in several parts of the United States. Its chief executive is Fred H. Vahlsing, a plump, cigar-smoking extrovert who overwhelms friend and foe alike with hearty handshakes and grinning good humor. If his social style is vintage Ring Lardner, his political stance is unorthodox in Maine, where industrialists habitually stand with the old-guard Republicans.

"Vahlsing certainly is prominent, embarrassingly prominent many say, in Democratic 'big occasions,' " columnist Bill Caldwell wrote several years ago in the *Maine Sunday Telegram*. "His planes and limousines dance attendance on Maine Democrats at conventions. His ringside tables at fund-raising

Democratic dinners are filled with Maine Democrats. His hospitality suites offer free food and drink for Maine Democrats. He is conspicuous as a 'big spender' for Democrats."

In 1960 "Freddie" Vahlsing applied for a license to discharge wastes from his new potato-processing plant at Easton into the Prestile. In his application he agreed to provide proper treatment before discharging wastes or "cease operation." The license was granted by the state. Theoretically, Vahlsing's plant was obliged to regulate its discharges to conform to the stream's B classification. (The state assigns each waterway in Maine a classification, ranging from A, which is fit for drinking, to D, which may be defined realistically as an open sewer; the Prestile's B classification certified its water as suitable for the propagation of fish, and, after treatment, for use as drinking water.) Vahlsing went into business, preparing a variety of potato products including frozen French fries, hash-browns, and other ready-to-use items. The waste parts, according to the license, were supposed to be treated before being discharged into the stream, a process that includes settling out the solids and treating the liquid residues with chemicals.

"We feel the same as you do, that these rivers and streams should be protected," Vahlsing told the state officials who had approved his application to discharge wastes into the Prestile. They took him at his word. But by 1962 fish were dying in increasing numbers in the once flourishing trout stream. Easton's summer swimming program was canceled. The Maine Water Improvement Commission (precursor to the Environmental Improvement Commission) reported that Vahlsing was providing "inadequate treatment" for the plant's wastes. Between that time and 1965 the WIC noted thirty-one violations of the stream's B classification by wastes from the Vahlsing plant. The Prestile's quality was B only on the WIC's books; in fact, it had become an open sewer.

"It's a dead stream," a Fish and Game Department official told a reporter. "It couldn't be any deader. You could grow better trout on the main street of Augusta than you could up there."

Vahlsing continued to deny the charges, contending that his waste-treatment plant was totally adequate. WIC technicians disagreed and said that the plant was not working properly because of bad design. Pressure began to build up on Vahlsing to mend his ways. The WIC asked the state's attorney general to take legal action against the company. Residents of Mars Hill, which lies below Easton on the Prestile, complained of the "nuisance conditions" created by the stream. The smell, they claimed, was intolerable, while the paint on their houses had blistered and blackened. The worst indignity of all was the realization that during the 1950s Mars Hill, with a population of only 2100 had been obliged by the state to assume an indebtedness of $260,000 in bonds to build a municipal sewage-treatment plant. The plant was designed to help upgrade the Prestile to a B classification. Local people circulated petitions through the town, asking the governor for relief. Because some of Mars Hill's residents were employed by Vahlsing, the sentiment against pollution there was by no means unanimous, and several copies are said to have been mysteriously destroyed. Nonetheless, 420 residents signed the petition.

Until this point the situation on the Prestile differed little from that on any other small waterway where pollution can be traced to a dominant (though not necessarily single) source. Justice may be expected to take its course if public opinion is insistent. But now another element entered the picture. It was created by Congress in the form of the Sugar Act of 1962, which provided for the expansion of sugar-beet production in various regions of the country. One of the regions in which Congress showed an interest was Maine's Aroostook County. Potato farming is considered a boom-or-bust business and government officials believed that sugar beets might stabilize agriculture in Aroostook County by giving local farmers an alternate crop. Under the terms of the Act, Maine was allotted

an annual crop of thirty-three thousand acres of sugar beets
and eight million dollars in loans to build a refinery in which
to process the beets.

Early in 1965 Vahlsing announced he would build just such
a refinery on the Prestile next to his potato-processing plant.
He named his new venture Maine Sugar Industries. The WIC
commented that a beet refinery might very well add to the
pollution problem created by Vahlsing's potato-processing
plant. But Maine's politicians came to Vahlsing's rescue. It
would be difficult for Vahlsing to receive loans to build the
refinery through the Maine Industrial Building Authority if he
were already in trouble with the state for polluting the
Prestile. A bill was introduced in the legislature to solve
Vahlsing's problem by lowering the Prestile's classification
from B to D. In that event, the legislature would be officially
confirming the stream's status as an open sewer and Vahlsing
would no longer be in the position of degrading it.

Flamboyantly, Vahlsing rallied the legislators. He brought
several hundred employees and supporters from Aroostook
County to a hearing on the bill at the state capital. Mrs.
Charles McEvoy, the president of the Maine League of
Women Voters, recalled Vahlsing's performance at the legisla-
tive hearing.

"Mr. Vahlsing admitted he expected to have his hands full
with technical problems in the first few years of operation of a
beet plant, and he didn't want to have to think about the
problems of sewage treatment," Mrs. McEvoy said. "In fact,
when pressed, he said it would be at least five years before he
could get around to it. He pleaded that if beets failed he might
be in the business of selling secondhand sugar-beet machinery
or a building, but that there wouldn't be much market for a
secondhand treatment plant. He was asking the state of Maine
to sacrifice a natural resource, to compromise its pollution
abatement program, in order to reduce the cost of a proposed
refinery and to reduce the loss if the plant should fail."

Conservationists who spoke against the bill at the hearing

found themselves subjected to Vahlsing's relentless charm. (Indeed, in a typically dashing gesture he offered to take all seventy-five members of the League of Women Voters delegation to lunch in order to explain his position. The ladies politely declined.) Early the following morning Vahlsing phoned Ezra James Briggs, a prominent Republican legislative leader in Maine and an outspoken opponent of the bill.

"I had never met the man," Briggs told me later. "But he got me out of bed with the introduction, 'Jim, this is Freddie.' Then he asked me if I would accept a position on the board of directors of his new sugar-beet company. I said no thanks, and went back to bed."

In the light of the eventual catastrophe, a number of Maine's leading politicians claimed the bill to lower the Prestile's classification was innocuous enough. They said it was done simply to insure that legal action could not be taken against Vahlsing if the sugar-beet refinery happened to pollute the stream during its shakedown period. This is nonsense, of course. The sugar-beet refinery could not degrade the Prestile's water below class B simply because that was already being done by the potato plant or other nearby sources. As the *Maine Times* said afterward, "The downgrading of the Prestile was needed not to aid the sugar-beet cause but to get Vahlsing off a legal hook because of the gross pollution by his potato-processing plant, which at the time was under threat of legal action by the attorney general's office."

Maine's Governor John H. Reed, a Republican, made an unusual appearance before a joint session of the legislature to ask for passage of the bill. Senator Muskie from his Washington office threw his support behind the bill, too; though he did extract from Vahlsing guarantees that the sugar-beet refinery would carry the finest treatment equipment available, the Senator would have cause later to regret that his name was associated with the bill.

The stakes were high. Vahlsing was reaching for millions of dollars in loans, which were to be guaranteed by the state. In a sense he put his life on the line: he took out a seven-million-dollar life-insurance policy from the Aetna Life Insurance Company to use as security for a part of the loans. An Aetna publicity man said that it was the largest policy the company had ever written for an individual. Vahlsing's furious activity was rewarded when the state legislature approved the bill, lowering the Prestile's classification to D as soon as the sugar-beet refinery opened.

Meanwhile, though the stream's B classification was not being met, the attorney general's office had difficulty in forcing Vahlsing to clean up the stream.

"A part of the legal problem I have with Vahlsing, Inc.," James S. Erwin, the attorney general, said, "is that the legislature has by statute exempted that firm (as well as many other major polluters in Maine) from prosecution for violation of water-quality classification as long as a statutory cleanup timetable is met. The outer limit of this timetable is 1976. As a result, I was forced in the case of Vahlsing, Inc., to resort to my common-law powers as guardian of the public welfare and sue to have the firm declared a 'public nuisance.' As any lawyer will tell you, there are precious few standards for determining what a 'public nuisance' is. It is also difficult for my office to attract and keep young lawyers to fight pollution when I must offer them so much less per year than the competing private law firms who represent the polluters."

The state's inaction was further explained by reporter Kenneth H. Morrison in the *Bath-Brunswick Times-Record*: "Various sources close to the situation at the time said that the state did everything possible to avoid a showdown with Vahlsing because the state was so heavily committed financially by backing loans for the potato processing plant as well as $8 million for the sugar refinery."

II ❧ CRITICISM of the whole affair began to mount as it became apparent that the pollution problem on the Prestile remained severe. By "legalizing pollution," Maine's politicians had betrayed the town of Mars Hill, whose investment in a sewage-treatment plant was now undone. Moreover, the pollution was not confined to Maine, but ultimately was being unloaded on the people of Canada. Even some of Vahlsing's most influential supporters began to change their stance. Foremost among them was Senator Muskie, whose call for "flexibility" in the reclassification of the Prestile had played a part in the legislature's vote. Speaking at the annual dinner of the Natural Resources Council of Maine, a private organization of conservationists, in 1965, Muskie attempted to defend himself against the charge that he had contributed to pollution in Maine.

"If I felt for one moment," he told the assembled conservationists, "that the sugar-beet refinery meant that the Prestile is condemned to a status of an open sewer, I would not have supported the proposal to reclassify the stream. The reclassification was intended to be temporary. It was designed to meet an immediate problem in connection with the financing of the plant."

As Muskie said, the reclassification was to be temporary, but the plan was to bring it back only as far as a class-C rating for the time being. This was, in fact, a retrogressive step on Muskie's part, for he had persistently advocated since his days as governor that each stream in Maine be raised, rather than lowered, in its quality rating. The little Prestile grew in stature as a public nuisance.

—

July 7, 1968, was a warm day in New Brunswick. As he went about his chores at home in Centreville, Bob Caines was mindful of the odor that reached him from the Prestile, half a mile away. He and his wife had never quite got used to it, though it was to be expected at that time of the year when the temperature rose and the stream's flow dwindled. But as the morning wore on the smell increased.

"I remember there was a knock on the door," Caines told me, "and when I opened it a couple of small boys were standing there with a bucket of dead fish. They wanted to sell me the lot of them for a dollar. The fish didn't smell very good so I asked the boys where they got them.

" 'We didn't catch them,' they told me. 'We picked them up beside the stream.' "

Caines got into his car and drove to the Prestile. There, along the stream's banks, he saw hundreds of rotting trout heaped in windrows. An official provincial report later described the situation. "This was perhaps the most complete fish kill which has ever occurred in the Province. Practically all fish life was eliminated in the main branch of the river from Easton, Maine, to its mouth at the St. John River, a distance of some 25 miles."

Caines drove back to his house, where he closed himself in from the smell and made some telephone calls. He tried unsuccessfully to persuade several New Brunswick officials to protest to their counterparts in Maine. Then he called friends in Centreville whom he knew to be as disgusted as he was by this latest indignity. Finally, he called a number of newspaper and television stations to make a startling announcement.

"The funny thing was we never intended to go through with the thing," Caines told me, overwhelmed by the recollection of his own audacity. "It was all a bluff on our part—and they called our bluff!"

The plan was this: Caines publicly stated an intention to build a dam across the Prestile. On the morning of July 8 Caines and his friends, two of whom provided bulldozers, would stage a show of force on the United States–Canada border. To lend a realistic note to their demonstration they would drive the bulldozers into the stream bed as if they intended to dam the Prestile and hurl the filth back upon the polluters in Maine. At this point, so they reasoned, the authorities would step in and demand that the demonstrators disperse. Being law-abiding citizens, they would obey the orders, leaving their point to be made by the assembled cameramen, whose pictures would illustrate how close reasonable men had been pushed to the point of anarchy.

"We showed up that morning to find crowds of people packed just inside the border," Caines said. "A customs officer told me later they had counted over six thousand people in the area that day. There were cameramen from Canada and from across the line. There were several more bulldozers than we'd planned on—five in all—with their operators anxious to start work. There were lots of people from both sides of the border just cheering us on. The Mounties were there. I was waiting for them to stop us, but they just went on directing traffic. What could we do but go ahead?"

And so the reluctant crusaders gouged out some earth from the banks with their bulldozers and piled it in the stream. By midafternoon an earthen dam ten feet high stretched one hundred feet, from bank to bank, across the Prestile.

"We were afraid that the stream was going to back up on the potato field that belonged to a nice fellow named Wallace Pryor, just the other side of the line," Caines recalls. "But he said he didn't mind, he lived along that stream, too, and he didn't like the smell of rotten potatoes any more than we did. 'Go to it,' he said, 'I've got other fields planted.' We finished at three o'clock that afternoon and then everybody went home."

They had created the nicest international incident imaginable.

"It was a beautiful sight to see," recalled one of the customs officers on the United States side. "The dam really worked. The water backed up as far as you could see, rising along the banks."

"Was the smell as bad as the people in Centreville said it was?" I asked him.

He nodded. "Sure was."

There was a flurry of excitement in Fredericton (the capital of New Brunswick province) and in Ottawa, Augusta, and Washington. The provincial authorities, unsettled by the militancy of their compatriots, made a show of concern.

"Do you realize you are violating at least four provincial and federal laws?" a member of the Water Improvement Authority asked Caines.

"When citizens have to do something like this to get the attention of you people," Caines retorted, "you ought to be ashamed of yourselves!"

Apparently they were. When Caines asked a Mountie why he and his colleagues had not interfered, the Mountie grinned.

"We had orders from Fredericton," he told Caines. "We weren't to interfere unless there was violence."

Caines and his friends removed the dam the next day. "We had made our point," Caines said. "Now we were just anxious to pull down the dam and let the backed-up flow come down and give the stream a good flushing."

Embarrassed officials on both sides of the border breathed a collective sigh of relief. If Augusta and Washington were in fact abetting Vahlsing, winking at his plant's effluent while lending him money, they could not very well make a show of indignation when citizens of a neighboring country took the law into their own hands. Canadian officials, though secretly delighted, were stalemated. Freddie Vahlsing, the center of the storm, pleaded that he had been a victim of an act of God: "Extremely low water levels." But the debate on the blighted stream would never be the same again.

III ❧ WHAT CAN WE SAY about the dam's aftermath? Well, for one thing, the Prestile's plight was publicized and the embattled Canadians received more widespread support. The Maine State Biologists Association announced a "boycott" of all Vahlsing potato products, but this scheme had a fatal flaw: Vahlsing sells most of his processed potato products to large companies which market them under their own labels. And no one was willing to tell the biologists under what brand names Vahlsing potatoes ultimately were sold. The boycott fizzled.

More tangible help came from Vahlsing himself, under prodding from the state, which had renewed its legal action.

"After bringing the action," Attorney General Erwin said, "we secured a court order allowing our engineers access to the Vahlsing premises to inspect its facilities. We found that Vahlsing had redesigned his waste-treatment facilities. No longer does he continually discharge mildly chlorinated potato wastes into the Prestile. Instead, he has constructed a large lagoon (over ten acres in surface area) to hold the waste and he pumps it from this lagoon through pipes to potato fields, where it is sprayed on the ground as fertilizer. We believe our court order precipitated this maneuver."

The quality of the stream's water grew distinctly better. The state decreed that its official classification would be raised over a period of years. But while matters improved on the Prestile, the residue in political Maine was acute embarrassment. The dream of a sugar-beet empire in northern Maine came apart in tatters. Aroostook potato farmers were generally unenthusiastic about planting part of their acreage in beets, they lacked experience, and new machinery proved too costly for many of them to buy. Drought ruined the already inadequate crop. Harsh words were leveled at Vahlsing by farmers who had not been paid for beets they had delivered to him. The town of

Easton refused Vahlsing's request for a tax abatement. Even worse for Vahlsing was that he was not able to make payments on his loans, the state had to assume responsibility for the eight-million-dollar indebtedness, and Maine Sugar Industries (Freddie Vahlsing, proprietor) found itself entangled in bankruptcy hearings.

The state legislature, dominated by Republicans, saw an opportunity to hang Vahlsing like an albatross around the necks of Maine Democrats. Vahlsing was "their" friend, the Republicans smirked as they pointed a finger at the Democrats and authorized an investigation into the circumstances behind the unfortunate loan to Maine Sugar Industries. (After much huffing and puffing, the inquiry uncovered no skullduggery.) Meanwhile, the Vahlsing enterprises continued to amass a great deal of unwelcome publicity in the various news media, publicity in which Senator Muskie was inevitably mentioned as a leading character (out of all proportion to the part he actually played, it might be said). Muskie suffered on in comparative silence for a while.

Early in 1970 my article on the Prestile was published in *American Heritage*. Believing as I did that Muskie's intervention in the affair, though ill-considered, was not of prime significance, I treated him in my article a lot more gently than had many members of the Maine press. I pointed out the Republican's complicity in the affair, both through the vote in the Republican-dominated legislature and the less-than-vigorous enforcement procedures put into effect by the Republican-dominated state administration. But, in the light of Chappaquiddick, Muskie had now become the Democrats' "front-runner" for the 1972 Presidential nomination. He grew extraordinarily sensitive to any criticism that might mar his image as the environment's "Mr. Clean." My article was apparently the breaking point for him. Other publications extracted my few mentions of Muskie and amplified them.

An editor at *American Heritage* phoned to tell me that Muskie was furious. Muskie had sent the magazine a draft of a letter protesting my article, which he asked the magazine to publish; the editor said that Muskie had not yet decided whether he would put his signature to the letter or let it appear over that of Don Nicoll, his administrative assistant. Evidently the famous Muskie temper was allowed to cool, for the letter when it appeared bore Nicoll's signature. It was a curious statement, dwelling on such already stated points as that (1) there had been pollution (Mars Hill sewage) of the Prestile before Vahlsing opened for business and (2) that the sugar-beet refinery had not become a source of pollution. The letter attempted to justify Muskie's intervention—though the state itself claimed that the potato-processing plant had violated antipollution regulations thirty-one times in the previous five years. Muskie seemed to be most upset because I had quoted a Portland newspaper's reference to his "friendship" with Vahlsing.

I called John Cole, the editor of the *Maine Times*. "You've been much tougher on Muskie than I have," I said. "And so have the other Maine papers. Have you heard of any other Muskie letters?"

"No," Cole said. "I guess he doesn't care what people in this state think. It's the national audience he's worried about now."

Boycotts, bankruptcies, and personal pique are matters of transient interest. It seems to me that the Prestile's chief interest is symbolic. It stands as an embarrassing reminder that eastern Maine and the Atlantic provinces are more closely tied together than they often care to admit. This tie will grow more binding in the light of the oil industry's interest in their common coastline.

PART ✠ FOUR
This Land Is Whose Land ?

11 THE
INTERNATIONAL
QUARTER

FOR THOSE of us who live in small Maine communities the annual "Town Report" makes better reading than a national news weekly. Here in different guises are the names of the people we see every day, appearing now as a tax delinquent, or as the town Health Officer filing her report on the state of our health, or as a man to whom the town owes a rebate of three dollars on his poll tax because he has passed his seventieth birthday. ("Him? Over seventy? Why, he doesn't look a day over fifty-five.") The people in the neighboring town of Columbia, though, must have different thoughts as they examine the list of tax delinquents in their "Town Report," for it reads like the telephone directory of a southern European town. Probably no other community in American can claim such a large percentage of alien taxpayers.

This, I thought when a friend showed me a copy of the "Columbia Town Report," looks like a clear case of absentee ownership. But who is being exploited? My friend suggested that I talk to Elwin Leighton, and I drove over to Columbia one morning while a wet snow fell on our part of the county. There is a lot of open country in Columbia, and one can mount its many low ridges and look out across thousands of acres of blueberry barrens and, farther north, to a vast heath (which always rhymes with "faith" in this part of the world).

Elwin Leighton lives in a sprawling, comfortable frame house on a sparsely settled road that wanders up toward the barrens and the heath. He is a short, barrel-chested man, a construction worker by trade and physique. It was a Sunday morning and he was preparing to leave for New Hampshire, where he worked five days of every week on the power line that will link the new Maine Yankee nuclear plant at Wiscasset, Maine, with other parts of the Northeast; there are very few big construction jobs to work on in Washington County. For a long time Elwin Leighton also had served as Columbia's tax collector, and it was in connection with those duties that I had come to see him.

"Tell me about Pine Island," I said as I settled into a rocking chair in his living room.

He ran a hand through his gray, crew-cut hair, thought for a minute, and then took out of a cabinet a map of the town and a large book in which he had kept his tax records.

"It all began back in the early 1960s when this fellow from Italy came to town looking for land to buy," he told me. "He came over here to see me a few times. Here's his name in this book—Elio Carerj, I'm not sure how to pronounce it. He spoke English with an accent, but not so bad I couldn't make him out."

Leighton pointed to the map, running his hand across an area dotted with those cryptic embryonic grassy plants that cartographers use to indicate heaths or bogs. "This through here is the heath, and this here is Pine Island. It's not really an island. It's just a piece of higher land in the middle of the heath, all covered with trees, mostly hardwoods. Well, this fellow bought Pine Island from an old man who lives over in

Harrington. It's about three hundred acres in all, and he paid a thousand dollars for it."

"Is there a road into Pine Island?" I asked him.

"No. This fellow was going to put in a road, but it would have been two or three miles through some woods and across the heath, which would have cost a lot of money. It's awful wet in there part of the year. The best time to go in is in the winter, when you can travel by snowmobile.

"But he spent quite a bit of money in there, anyhow, because he had Pine Island surveyed. I've seen the map he made up for the Registrar of Deeds in Machias. It looks awful pretty—it's all divided up into streets with names like Columbia Street and Sunset Avenue, and he's even got supermarkets and hot-dog stands and public buildings marked on there. It's quite a development. Only when you go up to Pine Island there's nothing there except a pile of street signs—all lettered and fastened on poles—that got tossed into the bushes."

With his paper development a gridwork of streets and boulevards, into which several hundred half-acre lots had been worked, Elio Carerj proceeded to set up shop in Europe. Columbia's tax records indicate that he found over 150 people eager to buy their piece of the New World, and some of them invested in two, three, or four lots. The town has a copy of one of the deeds that Carerj sent to a man in Milan, which describes his lot:

Bounded as follows:
On the north by Newark Street
On the east by lot n. 2 (Block 14)
On the west by Sunset Avenue

Elwin Leighton thumbed through the pages of his tax book. Among the Leightons and Grants and Nicholses there were the names of 138 landowners still in good standing whose home addresses were listed as Rome, Milan, Naples, Rapallo, Verona, Mantua, Bolzano, Pavia, Venice, Genoa, Munich, and a smattering of other places in Bavaria. Each half-acre lot is taxed by Columbia at $2.52.

"The town isn't getting rich from Pine Island," Elwin Leighton said with a straight face. "Most of these people pay their taxes every year, but some of them wrote to complain that we were listing them delinquent when they weren't getting their bills in time to meet the deadline, so now we have to send them air mail. That costs us twenty cents a letter, and then there's some extra correspondence and legal fees connected with it."

"Can you read their letters?" I asked him.

"No, not if they're in Italian. But there's a fellow over at the Naval Base at Winter Harbor that somebody told us about, and he translates the letters for us."

One letter in the tax book was written in English by a man who lives on the Via Francesco Ferrara in Rome:

> I wonder if you can give me some information about these lots. When my friends and I bought these lots, we were told that soon the seller was going to build sewers, streets, etc. Do you know if these works have been done? Pictures were shown to us demonstrating that trees were knocked down to build streets and sewers. If I am not troubling too much, I would like you to give us some information about this future housing development.

Elwin Leighton shrugged and tossed the letter back onto the table with the tax rolls.

"Well," he said, "if one of these people comes over to look at this housing development he's going to have a lot of company up there. That's where the black flies and mosquitoes breed by the billions."

People in Rapallo or Bolzano are not alone in their hankering for a piece of America's vacationland. For many Americans the "second home" is a vehicle by which they hope to recapture some part of their earlier years, lived more often than not in a community whose structure was comprehensible to its residents. Their home town, its government, and its social hierarchy likely fitted a familiar mold. Now the small towns have been largely abandoned, or they have been inundated by that overflow from the cities which has blurred municipal distinctions and left them with no sense of identity. What fascinated sociologists originally called Megalopolis lies spread out along the middle Atlantic coast from north of Boston to south of Washington like some gouged and formless creature flung up by the sea; on a second, closer look, the experts are pinning it with more appropriate names—"pathopolis" or "that urbanoid mishmash."

There has always been a seasonal exodus from the cities, and even from the suburbs. But formerly it was customary to rent a place in the country or at the shore for a couple of weeks during the summer, renewing the lease there the following year or drifting on to someplace else. Other people preferred to camp in distant regions of lakes and forests, and in recent years the numbers of Americans using state and national parks on their vacations has created scenes in these once-refreshing oases that resembled the congested "urbanoid mishmash" that the vacationers fled from in the first place. In 1968 visitors to the areas supervised by the National Park Service reached 150 million; people were turned away from the parks' campgrounds and thousands of automobiles clogged the parks' highways. At Yosemite National Park in California the authorities prohibited automobile traffic in a part of the famous valley. Attempts to discourage the flow of tourists into the national parks were resisted by local people who had adapted themselves to the tourist business. An old man who lives near one of the great national parks has summed up the economic benefits of that kind of land use by remarking, "One hundred tourists equal the income from one acre of potatoes, and are a damn sight easier pickin'!"

The reverberations set in motion by this swelling tide of people who are looking for their own special kinds of surcease from care simply boggle the mind. Hippies, for instance, fleeing the noise, filth, and fuzz of the cities, have carried their own noise and filth to rural areas (remember Woodstock!) or the national parks, and in some cases have sufficiently antagonized the rangers to set off head-breaking incidents among the evergreens and waterfalls. Urban areas, desperate for recreation space, often find it is unavailable. In Connecticut not long ago an assistant professor of public health at Yale University charged that the state's health commissioner was keeping badly polluted beaches open to avert violence in the slums.

"As a professional health official, he knows he should close the beaches for swimming," Eric Mood told the press after he had testified at a public hearing concerned with the pollution of Long Island Sound. "But as a humanitarian he knows that the socially deprived residents of his city have no other convenient outdoor bathing area to which they may seek relief from the oppressing summer heat of the urban slums in which they live. Should he close the beach and incur the wrath of the people kept out? The long hot summer is ahead of us, and it is principally the blacks who are affected, because so many lack transportation to get to beaches away from the polluted harbor."

It seemed not too long ago that there were more than enough shorelines in the world to hold everyone who wanted to dive into the surf and lie on the sand or poke about in the tide pools. In fact, our ancestors even looked on the sea and its edges as a place of terror. To northern people, the shore was a place to be avoided except by very queer souls or by those who made their living from some contact with the sea. It was only during the early eighteenth century in England, for instance, that people began to flock to such places as Brighton for "medicinal purposes," and once they found out the terrors had been exaggerated they began to flock to the shore for pleasure, too. Now, so heavy is the congestion, we no longer think of "medicinal" benefits from the shore, but will settle for polluted stretches of it.

And very often it is the beaches themselves that suffer most. Hawaii's Waikiki serves as an unsettling example of man's inhumanity to his surroundings. Once one of the world's loveliest and most famous beaches, Waikiki fell victim to the developer's greed and became a nightmare of chintzy hotels piled one upon another, so that whatever charm once lured people there from thousands of miles away has been utterly destroyed. Hawaii is now in the throes of trying to shackle the developers so that they will not destroy what is left of the islands.

"If someone designed a flag for the state for the 1960s," a Hawaiian official says, "it would be a speculator on a field of bucks."

If a man were putting in jeopardy only his own future well-being one might shrug off his destructive hijinks with the remark that it is nothing less than he deserves. But, like rats and cockroaches, man adapts quickly to the nightmare world he has created, while other creatures lapse into oblivion. This is what is happening in Hawaii, where one of the most unfortunate aspects of man's development schemes is a withering away of the islands' once marvelous diversity. Paul M. Scheffer, Hawaii's state conservationist, reports that the mass extinction of bird life in an area of that size is unequaled anywhere in the world; more than half the birds that are threatened with extinction in the United States are natives of Hawaii. Twenty-seven of seventy species native to Hawaii have become extinct since 1778, and nineteen others are listed among the nation's endangered birds. Scheffer predicted "catastrophic consequences resulting from the destruction or alteration of the native birds' habitats."

Sometimes the destruction of the landscape seems insignificant to "objective" observers. Ada and I have often stayed at a friend's cottage on Florida's northern Gulf coast. It is in a lovely setting, perched high on the dunes overlooking the Gulf, and one can walk into the dunes away from the shore and at each turn come upon some long-legged bird or a feeding animal or a wild flower that is unfamiliar to a Northerner's eyes. On a trip to the South recently, I saw our friend and asked her how things were at her cottage.

"I'm getting awful discouraged," she said. "People are coming down from Georgia and Alabama now on weekends with their dune buggies, and they're just driving up and down on the dunes all day long. They're wearing down the dunes, and tearing up the plants that hold the dunes together, and the wind comes along and blows the sand away, and you can just see those dunes disappearing right in front of your eyes."

"Well, so what?" our objective observer might remark. "There are plenty of dunes left. Why get excited about what's happening on some isolated stretch of the Gulf coast?"

But the point is that all of us, on whatever coast and on whatever mountain, are able to supply our own examples of this sort of thing. The destruction, on the face of it, seems local and minor, but it is being repeated every day and endlessly— all of us meet it in one form or another. In their total effect, these million little assaults on the environment are depressing to people who care, and devastating to the environment.

Consider France, where the developers are carving up the Alps to build resorts and skiing areas, altering the communities of grasses and trees and ultimately, so their opponents say, triggering disastrous avalanches. Here in the United States the expanding winter-recreation industry may eventually rival its summertime counterpart in mistreating the land.

Meanwhile, the remote countryside that was being abandoned to nature's regenerative forces suddenly has found a host of new admirers. Parcels of its land, still comparatively cheap and blessed with air and water that is still comparatively pure, are now deemed desirable. The buyers are lining up. In America's erstwhile backwaters—Montana, the mountains of the Southwest, and northern New England—lies the promise of a second home, or even a brand-new one.

12
LAND BOOM

THERE HAS BEEN a steady migration into Maine for some years. At first it was made up mostly of men and women who were coming back to the ancestral homestead or retired couples who were fulfilling an old dream and, disdaining Florida's sybaritic ease, craved like Robert Frost "the sweet of bitter bark and burning clove." But the median age of immigrants to eastern Maine has dropped sharply in the last ten years, and many of them are young people just out of college or refugees from communes in New York and California.

The lure is cheap land and a satisfying way of life. If the newcomers don't demand shore property, the first goal is still easier to come by than the second. Several years ago a young couple we know bought sixty acres of woodland—bisected by a swift-running stream, within sight of salt water—for six hundred dollars. Another couple bought three hundred acres a few miles inland for about eight dollars an acre. All of these young friends of ours are college graduates and from well-to-do families, the young men strong and able to work hard with their hands, the women equipped to teach and thus help out in lean times. They built their own houses. They have survived here because they hold no illusions about the land. Though both couples raise much of their own food in garden plots, they were quick to adapt their energy and their skills to local conditions. The men have earned their living chiefly by fishing, carpentry, and working part-time for the owners of a large farm in the area.

Others arrive with stars in their eyes. A resident hereabouts is Scott Nearing, whose books about independence and the good life stirred atavistic desires in a good many people during the 1930s. Nearing lived in Vermont at the time, and his ideas about subsistence farming were relevant. He has moved to the Maine coast since then and his books have experienced a considerable revival among today's alienated young people. Many of them come to sit at the feet of the master, then set out to clear their newly bought piece of woodland and live happily ever after on the good earth's bounty.

The trouble is that the Maine earth is niggardly. Its price may be cheaper than the land farther south, but its soil is poor, especially along the coast. The last of the great glaciers of post-Pleistocene times scraped the underlying granite clean. Whatever soil has accumulated here is of recent geological origin, thin and deficient in nutrients. The growing season is short; a man who puts his young tomatoes out early is likely to have them nipped by late-spring frost, yet if he waits for warmer weather the fruit may be hit still unripened by the first frost of late summer. Even during the best of summers the aspiring subsistence farmer fights a losing battle today. His father could get by in a barter economy thirty years ago, but the son finds it not so easy to persuade a merchant to exchange a needed piece of machinery for a chicken and two dozen eggs. The cost of maintaining an automobile has destroyed subsistence farming: a man once could count on the fruits of the land to cover the care and feeding of a horse. "But Scott Nearing makes out," the hopeful farmer persists. Yes, and Scott and Helen Nearing are elderly vegetarians with no children and a steady income now from their books and lectures. Around January there is generally an exodus among the young; a few couples go back to San Francisco and the next summer the alders begin to reclaim the scar in the woods that had been an incipient cornfield.

Young professionals come to buy the land and live here, too, though the drift is not so apparent. Like most rural areas, ours needs another doctor. A bright young doctor just detached from Navy duty came here to practice temporarily a year or two ago and appeared likely to settle down. But his wife felt the starkness and they chose Arizona instead. Other young professionals make a place for themselves here, often at a considerable financial sacrifice. A young professional woman captured by the state's beauty now dreads even the thought of her periodic holiday visits to her family's home in the South.

"The only practical way for me to travel home on a short holiday is by plane, and I was never scared of them before," she told me. "But now all the time I'm on the plane I'm scared to death it's going to crash. I love this place so damn much that I'm terrified something will happen to me *outside of Maine*."

Not everyone who comes to stay sees eastern Maine in such a pure light. A Jew, who has spent most of his life in New York City but who bought a home here after we helped him and his wife rent a place nearby one summer, remains enchanted, with but a single complaint: "I hunger for some *profiles*," he says, after staring at Down East faces all day. Other people's complaints, it seems to me, are self-defeating. They praise the views and the seabreezes, but they cannot forgive the local people their snowmobiles, their shootin' irons, and even their mobile homes.

Naturally, this breeds a good deal of hard feeling. Summer's lease is all too short in this part of the world, and snowmobiling and hunting help to beguile the tedium of the colder months for a great many people; in an area where housing is often substandard, with tarpaper shacks apparent in the countryside, mobile homes mean a lot to some local people during the long winters, being the most livable shelters they have ever had.

Yet Maine's population has remained comparatively static. There has been a steady "out-migration" of young people in search of jobs, barely overcome in recent years by births and immigration. The 1970 Census revealed that the state's population had crept past the million mark (1,006,320), an increase of 3.8 per cent since 1960. This increase is insignificant when compared with that of another "vacationland," Florida, which was 34.7 per cent, or even those of the neighboring New England states of New Hampshire (21.5) and Vermont (14.1). In eastern Maine there continues to be a net loss. Washington County, where I live, includes 2420 square miles, which is larger than Delaware, yet fewer than 30,000 people live here; the population declined 11 per cent between 1960 and 1970. Traditionally, land has been available, but the region's isolation and the policy of the landowners has tended to keep people out.

The sea has always been the most logical route into eastern Maine, sailing "down east" from Boston before the prevailing wind. Both freight and tourists arrived at Maine towns by coastal schooners and steamers, the "rusticators" bringing their children, their servants, and their elaborate luggage with them for the summer holidays. For a while railways moved in as a supplemental means of transportation, opening up new areas of the state to those in search of peaceful retreats. Bar Harbor became the most fashionable summer resort in eastern Maine, with the Rockefellers and other wealthy families buying up the available land on Mount Desert Island. But all along the coast one can still see those rambling old "cottages" clustered on various necks and points where the large families of the day enjoyed their holidays. On Mount Desert Island, much of the land was taken out of circulation permanently when the wealthy families pooled some of their holdings and donated it to the federal government as a nucleus for Acadia National Park. Thus, while the other tourist colonies decayed with the Depression and the decline of coastal and railway transportation in the state, Bar Harbor retained some of its prosperity, as the local people who had farmed the land or served the wealthy summer people turned to the tourist business.

Not even the advent of the automobile brought eastern Maine as close to the great population centers as it had been in the days of coastal travel. An old woman in our town once told me about a trip home from Brooklyn, New York, where she had gone to do her student nursing before World War I. One of the doctors at the hospital where she trained owned a summer place here, and he agreed to drive her and several other nurses to Maine for their summer vacations. "The first night we made it to Yonkers," she told me. "A headlamp fell off there. We had flat tires, too, all along the way and it took us six days to arrive."

This isolation made it nice for the painters, of course, once they got here. They painted unspoiled landscapes, quaint fishing villages, and old waterfronts tinged with decay. But for most people the summer-long vacations in large cottages, and the servants that were needed to take care of them, had become a thing of the past. Gradually, the cottages were abandoned; some burned, and their owners did not return to rebuild.

Elsewhere, the land is coming under a variety of pressures. While taxes on the woodlands in unorganized areas (where there are no organized towns) are set by the state, the land in organized towns is taxed by the local authorities. Assessment is often a haphazard affair, responding to a town's financial needs of the moment. In some places the "summer people" bear the local tax burden, in other places the emphasis has been placed on its "potential" use, no matter who owns the land. Thus a man who operates a tree farm within an organized town may be taxed at the rate of two dollars an acre because his land happens to be near an area that is being profitably developed; since growing trees is a time-consuming process, with perhaps fifty to sixty years between harvests, economists have estimated that the return on woodlands comes to only a little over a dollar a year.

In similar trouble, taxed beyond its capacity to produce because of its superb location, is the salt-water farm that once was one of the coast's glories:

The farm for boys to grow up on
Is one where seagulls bring the dawn
*Over early on their wings.**

And as the original owners of the old farms and woodlands were forced into selling, the buyers arrived on the highways that have brought even eastern Maine within only a long day's drive of New York City. In fact, other parts of Maine are now within a day's drive of fifty million people who stretch in a great arc through the densely populated Northeast from Washington, D.C., to Cleveland. The people come as tourists; some buy land to remain part-time as summer people; and some of the latter group begin to use the plot they originally bought as a summer home more and more often on holidays and weekends throughout the year. These people aren't counted as residents, but the pressures in service and land usage they are beginning to put on the state is considerable.

Dr. Donaldson Koons of the state's Board of Environmental Protection has estimated that the land-development business in Maine is operating at a gross rate of a billion dollars a year. Accurate figures are difficult to come by, but Koons' information suggests that the land sold each year is valued at three hundred million dollars, and the rest of the sum is made up by construction.

"I've sold only one house in a year, and that had fifty acres

* "A Boy on a Saltwater Farm," from *Saltwater Farm*, by Robert P. Tristram Coffin, The Macmillan Company, New York, 1937.

of land with it," a friend of mine in the real-estate business here told me recently. "Everybody wants *land*. The people in town don't understand that. They think just because they have a nice house they can put it up for sale and get twenty-five thousand dollars for it. Maybe some places they can, but not here. The owners don't understand that the people coming here want privacy. They don't want to buy a house on Main Street—that's what they've got back in the suburbs."

And so, a couple from "away" will buy a ramshackle old house that a self-respecting local person wouldn't stick a horse into, because it stands at the end of a lonely road or in the midst of a broad meadow. It's just like a man fancying himself very comfortable in the sort of room in Paris that he would shun in, let's say, Akron, Ohio.

A long-held conviction here that outsiders are a little queer is compounded now by darker suspicions: the state's attorney general articulated the feeling a year or two ago when he announced that the Mafia stands behind many of the land-development schemes that have cropped up in Maine. Today the community is all abuzz if a man who looks like George Raft comes to town and asks about a piece of property.

That hanky-panky flourishes is common knowledge. There are titillating newspaper reports about Maine land of dubious quality being sold at auction in dimly lit hotel rooms in Boston. Although the state requires certain standards for those developments on land measuring twenty acres or more, the developers often evade the law by bringing four brothers-in-law, or other confederates, in on the deal to split the land into "separate" units. The *Maine Times*, a useful weekly newspaper, has acted as something of a watchdog over the brasher development schemes.

One of the developers whose career the *Maine Times* has followed assiduously is a Massachusetts man named Charles Geotis (who has also gone about his business under such aliases as Charles Endicott and even Charles G. Otis). Though Geotis was indicted by both the state and federal attorneys in connection with several of his land schemes, he pointed out that he was simply working in "the American way." Geotis entered the market looking for land that was suitable for his purposes—if not for many others'. Once he divided the land, preferably near a lake since seashore property had grown too expensive for his sort of operation, he proceeded to attract buyers who were interested in a "second home." One of his methods was to hand out certificates printed to resemble checks and which he described as being worth five hundred dollars toward the purchase of one of his lots. The half-acre lots, for which he asked a thousand dollars an acre, have often been described by his critics as unsuitable for buildings and sewage facilities because of their poor soil. Geotis argued, undeniably, that he was selling land and not houses.

"A person might not build on one of those lots for twenty years," he told Peter Cox of the *Maine Times*. "He might just want to put up an easel and paint there. . . . When he does build, technology might have solved the pollution problem. If this country can build the hydrogen bomb, it should be able to figure out how to take apart a turd."

Geotis, to his sorrow, was not able to figure out how to evade the authorities. The federal government accused him of selling lots in a "luxury development" which he never had any intention of developing and he was convicted in a U.S. District Court of using the mails to commit "frauds and swindles."

In the light of studies made by the Soil Conservation Service of the United States Department of Agriculture, it is interesting to speculate that Geotis is not a social phenomenon but simply one of a common breed who happened to be singled out for attention. According to the SCS, less than fifteen per cent of Maine's land is suitable for the installation of septic tanks, which are the favored means of waste disposal for most of the state's rural homes and vacation cottages. In the remaining eighty-five per cent, the soils are disqualified for this use, being poorly drained or excessively drained, in either case contributing to the contamination of the ground water or nearby lakes and streams.

The land around Maine's lakes is beginning to come under as much pressure as that along the seashore. People want to spend their vacations near water, and they will readily accept fresh water when they are crowded off the edge of the sea. This is especially true in Maine, where the coldness of the ocean water (about fifty-five degrees at the peak of summer), the uncertain winds, and the rise and fall of the tides send many people inland for their boating and swimming. Although Ada and I live on the salt water and own a couple of small boats, we bought a canoe several years ago to be able to take advantage of the good weather inland on the rivers and lakes when fog or high winds blanket the coast.

Developers cluster their camps around the inland lakes. This "cluster development," recommended in places where it is desirable to set aside ample open space by restricting buildings to a small area of the available land, is favored by the lake developers simply because the lots up front bring the highest prices. This policy makes it inevitable that sewage contaminates the water or stimulates the growth of algae to an extent that it smothers the fish and other aquatic organisms.

A more costly status symbol is an island home. There are probably a thousand islands along the Maine coast large enough to support vegetation. The largest of them were among the first inhabited portions of the state, since they provided an excellent base from which to fish, as well as a refuge during the Indian wars. Even those islands that have never been lived on have been used by the coastal people for centuries as convenient grazing grounds (no fences are required) for their sheep. It still gives one a start today to cruise past an isolated offshore island and see a flock of sheep grazing on its grass and shrubs or poking about the rockweed on the shore at low tide.

Recently a real-estate man in mid-coast Maine said that a

large island, measuring perhaps half a mile long on each side, sold for ten thousand dollars in 1946, though today it would be difficult to find one for sale even at five hundred thousand. Islands in that area ordinarily sell for about three thousand dollars an acre. On our part of the coast the price is closer to one thousand dollars an acre, and the demand is high. This seems curious at first because in many cases these islands remain status symbols rather than sites of summer homes. Unless they are close to shore, they are difficult to reach and land on in rough weather, while many of the offshore islands lack both trees and fresh water.

A natural treasure that is jeopardized by this rush for remote islands is Maine's large population of nesting sea birds. The islands have offered protection from predation by humans and other mammals to terns, guillemots, petrels, and other species which need such seclusion to reproduce successfully year after year. Technology may provide some yet unimagined solutions to the current transportation problems, which will undoubtedly add another threat to these birds which are already reeling under a variety of other man-made ills.

"I think at that time we'll have to provide for some sort of cluster development on the outer islands," says ornithologist William H. Drury, Jr., who has studied sea birds on the Maine coast for many years. "Instead of letting one or two families inhabit each island, a practice that will inevitably ruin critical nesting areas, it would be better to cram people on just a few of those islands, as they used to do in fishing villages."

The rush for remote islands is not so curious, at that. One of those barren islands, its rocks spattered white with bird droppings and its rocky rim sculptured by the fierce northern seas, may symbolize better than anything else these days the second homes that Americans are looking for. It is a little bit like the "desert island" that earlier generations dreamed of before the Hiltons of our world took them all over as sites for their resort hotels. (Some men seem to have been born just to exploit the dreams of their fellows.) But no ingratiating hotelkeeper has yet started to bulldoze the small outer islands Down East. In buying a second home or a plot of isolated land, then, we are acting out the old dream of turning our backs on the miserable world that we and our fellows have made, and in which we feel ourselves trapped.

13

STEWARDSHIP

ONE OF THE strongest human desires is to possess land. Aristocrats, bourgeoisie, proletarians, peasants—the urge comes in season. Even today, among my friends who have been committed for many years to life in apartments, the desire to own a house seems to be stirring. Admittedly, this does not always reflect a hunger for the land itself, but rather it is a desperate reach to defend themselves; they want to stay in the city and buy a brownstone to protect themselves against rapacious landlords, or flee to a suburban home to protect themselves against the city's various hobgoblins.

So the ownership of land does not necessarily instill the idea of stewardship. Just as the most ferocious cruelty to animals (and even to children!) is found among those with legal claims to them, so the worst abuses on the land often are traced to those who own it. "It's my land, and nobody is going to tell me how to use it!" is a comment that generally bodes no good to the land in question, or to neighboring land, either. Concern for the land often manifests itself simply as a fear that neighborhood property values will decline if such-and-such happens. Conversely, anything that promises to lift property values is welcomed, even though the character or the quality of the land is destroyed. Remember that in many cases it was the people who owned the unique saw grass and cypress country near Everglades National Park who promoted the idea to build a jetport there—and, had it succeeded, it would ultimately have destroyed the Park. And remember, too, it is the farmers and other landowners who turn over their land to stripminers in exchange for royalties; the strippers gouge out the coal, then turn back to its owners, along with mining royalties, the ravaged land that will be no good to man or beast for decades to come.

But to other men and women the land offers something more than simply a chance to speculate. Because their plot of land represents the earth that sustains us all, these people find in it certain spiritual values that transcend the ones they find in any other "real" property, including those properties made up of many symbolic levels such as books and works of art: "But the earth abideth forever." Obviously these feelings were in abeyance during the century or so when Americans were "conquering" their land. But they are rising to the surface again, and now there even seems to be little distinction between reverence for one's own little plot and for the landscape that stretches beyond it.

The experience of buying our own land and putting back into shape the old house that stood on it has, for Ada and me, a meaning beyond what is personal in any transaction of that sort. It bound us to a special part of America, and threw us into what we like to think of in our more euphoric moments as the "crusade" to preserve it from those who would do it harm. This experience, I also believe, is one that is becoming a common bond among Americans of whatever region, and in that sense it is a part of this book.

I don't want to give the impression that such a transaction

was easy, even at the beginning of the 1960s when we made up our minds to buy land and make our future in eastern Maine. The coast in Washington County, though happily it was (and still is) largely in the hands of the people who live here, was often unavailable for one reason or another. Owners clung to unused property out of sentiment, inertia, or the hope that prices would rise, as they very soon did. We found that in many cases the land had been divided among so many relatives ("heirship property," it is called) or the title to the land had grown so fuzzy that the most logical owner was in effect paralyzed, unable to accept a valid offer. We visited lovely old houses, unlived in, that were rotting away, their once-magnificent views now closed off by untended vegetation. The land itself along the coast was often for sale, great chunks of it, and at reasonable prices, but houses in striking locations, no. We had our hearts set on an old house, a desire that many of the old-time residents thought to be an aberration.

"Buy the land and build yourself a house," they would say. "Then you can have it the way you want it."

We did find a house, in fine condition but neither very new nor very old, in the location we wanted. It sat on a hillside overlooking the bay, a cluster of white birches in the clearing in front of it, and isolated from the road by a long lane and twenty acres of woodland. The house was ready for year-round living, with water, a furnace, furniture, and a large barn adjacent to it. The owners (people from away) were asking sixteen thousand five hundred dollars. A complication arose, however, when I went to the bank for a mortgage. One of the bank's directors, a man with considerable experience in business and politics, recommended against it.

"I'm doing you a favor," he told me. "That place—the house and barn and twenty acres and all—isn't worth ten thousand dollars, and I've told the owner so. We don't believe in prices like that around here."

We accepted his advice and kept looking.

When we bought our house and land it was, almost literally,

on a moment's notice. Jack Burke, who manages the local lobster pound, told us about it when we stopped there one afternoon to buy lobsters. The owner was a woman whose husband, a retired Marine, had just died. He had come to the Maine coast to rough it, getting along without an indoor toilet or running water for the six months of the year they lived there, but since he had a heart condition it fell to his wife to haul water from the neighbors' house and attend to all the other chores associated with roughing it. After his death, she wanted out.

We learned that she would be leaving for her daughter's home in another state early the next morning. We looked at the house and its setting, made up our minds at once, and paid a visit to friends in town to see if her asking price (less than half what was asked for the other place) was reasonable.

"Well, a house that don't have water isn't a house at all," one of our friends said, "but there's twenty acres of prime shore property with the house, and that by itself is worth the price she wants."

At six-thirty the next morning we went to her house with the down payment. (At the time we didn't even know that we would be able to get a mortgage for the rest, but we weren't going to turn back at this point.) She had roused her lawyer from bed to be there; and he, poor man, had not been able to locate a typist at that hour to prepare the necessary documents so had written them out himself by hand. Before breakfast we were well on the way to possession of our portion of the Maine coast.

The house we bought is an old (circa 1840) Cape Cod, standing on high ground that slopes down to the water where the Narraguagus River blossoms out into the bay. Later we learned that the land was part of a Revolutionary War grant to a local man who had served against the British. The old people knew how to choose their building sites. It is said in town that this dwelling's predecessor on the spot, in unconscious partnership with its neighbor across the river, turned back a probing British warship one dark night in 1812. When the would-be invaders detected lights on both sides of the river's mouth, they mistook them for a pair of forts and prudently withdrew. It is comforting to have a legend, instead of bats and termites, come with an old house.

Spread before us are the glories that the Maine coast is celebrated for, and which a new day threatens. Thickly wooded islands create a compelling intricacy in the bay both for sailors and idling landlubbers. On the mainland across from us the houses stand out at leisurely intervals in their clearings, each, as Van Wyck Brooks said of New England farmhouses, "belonging to the ground on which it stood, as a caterpillar belongs to the leaf on which it feeds." Not all of the houses are elegant, and one or two perhaps are a little the worse for wear, but none of them is ugly or pretentious. Cold, clean (or nearly so) water laps at the sturdy rocks beneath them. On sunny days the freshly painted lobster boats, so bright against the blue water they dazzle the eye, crisscross the bay. On other days fog like white wool muffles the islands in the distance. One sees eagles, ospreys, herons, ducks, loons, plovers, and sandpipers over the bay in their seasons. Gulls fly purposefully down the bay at sunset. Seals bask on isolated ledges.

Sink roots! That's the standard admonition to the landless, urging them to hie themselves to the nearest real-estate dealer. When we bought our place the admonition took on a certain literalness, for the roots we sank were a well and a cellar. A well in itself has spiritual overtones that lift it above utility, a quality that many people today find only in their automobiles. Perhaps it is the well's biblical associations, perhaps the well symbolizes our tapping of the earth to make it surrender the source of life to us. Compounding this image for me were memories of my childhood when we lived for a time during the Depression years with my great-aunt in Connecticut. The little boy I played with lived on a farm. After a run in the woods on a warm day, I always looked forward to getting back to his house, where we drew a dripping wooden bucket up from the inky depths of the well and slaked our thirst with that marvelous water.

I was in for something of a shock. The creation of a modern artesian well is more akin to drilling for oil than to the re-enactment of a biblical drama. The well drillers appeared on the scene with heavy vehicles and towering rigs and began their work, at six dollars a foot. I was told to expect them to hit water in less than 100 feet. But that minimum was reached and passed and still the drill droned on. Water appeared in dribbles, but never gushes. I felt as if I were sitting in a taxicab, being taken on an endless trip while the tab rose higher with each click of the meter. I had to get out of the house and go for long drives. One day the dribble increased to the satisfaction of the well driller. The depth had reached 320 feet, but now we owned a house with running water.

The cellar proved to be an even more grueling experience. When we bought the house, there was a small cellar under the living room, a clammy hole with a dirt floor and rocks drooping and askew in its rear wall. Elsewhere the house stood on rocks and squat posts just far enough off the ground so that a small animal could squeeze under it (when we excavated, we found the skeleton of a cat beneath the ground floor). A cellar and a foundation would do much to keep out winter cold, and would allow us to install a furnace.

To have a cellar gouged out under an old house is an ordeal, like an extremely harrowing operation on the stomach or intestines. The process is to remove all of the earth from beneath the house, meanwhile propping it up on jacks and piers of heavy beams as you go along. The first obstacle appeared when the contractor's crew attempted to tunnel under the house with a backhoe from the north side but found a solid ledge three feet below the floor. Blasting, of course, was out of the question. The ledge conclusively established the cellar's depth on that side of the house. The backhoe assaulted the other side, while a small crew was sent in with pick and shovel to excavate down to the ledge.

At that time I did my writing in a room on the north side just above the point where the crew was at work with pick and shovel. I would hear them turn one of the jacks, while simultaneously the old beams around me groaned piteously. I would rush outside for a word with the contractor. After extracting his assurance that he supervised every turn of the jack so that the house would not be twisted out of shape, I would return to my typewriter. A few minutes later I would overhear, like Hamlet at graveside, the voices of the diggers below me.

FIRST VOICE: Why do you suppose they plastered the inside before they put a cellar under the place?

SECOND VOICE: Beats me.

FIRST VOICE: Did you see what happened to the plaster in that place we lifted up in Harrington?

SECOND VOICE: Yep.

Off I would go again in search of an assuring word from our contractor.

At last the house, reasonably intact, its swaybacked floors still swaybacked, stood in the yawning pit with only jacks and piers to keep it from tumbling in. Ada was certain the chimney was going to fall out through the bottom of the house. Our only contact with the world around us was a board that stretched across the moat from our back door to solid ground. In the midst of this operation I had to fly to New York to see an editor. I prepared to leave for the Bangor airport before dawn one morning. The weather was miserable, an icy rain descending in sheets. I put on my L. L. Bean hunting shoes, with their rubber soles, and stepped out the back door. The next thing I knew I was hanging upside down by one foot, my head in the void beneath the house.

Apparently, the construction crew, when leaving the day before, had laid across the moat a board which happened to have a long nail sticking up through it. When I left the house in the dark, I stepped out onto the nail. This caused me to stumble, overturning the board, and since the nail penetrated into the thick rubber sole of my boot I was flung into the pit, one foot fastened to the board, which remained wedged between the house and the solid ground on the other side. My cries for help were drowned by the tempest. Ada slept peacefully on. It was five minutes before I managed to kick my shoe (water all the time dripping into my nose and eyes) loose from the nail and pull myself up out of the muddy pit. I set out for the airport in a mood as foul as the weather.

The house withstood the ordeal better than we did. Today we live in it more comfortably than any of our predecessors, thanks in part to the oil that heats it. (Even conservationists look kindly on oil itself, if not on the careless way it is shipped and refined.) Our predecessors here smashed glass bottles on the shore and, acting from inclinations of sport or animosity, shot all the wild animals around the place. But they did not use any oil. Perhaps the only certified fact is not that the Maine coast is changing hands for the better, but that it is changing hands.

That much is certain. Not long ago I overheard two men who had come to the house to make some repairs I was not clever enough to handle myself. They were standing on the front lawn, talking about the view down the bay.

"Ain't it pretty, though?" one of the men commented.

The other nodded. "You know, when we owned the shore property we never thought nothin' about it," he said. "Now we don't own it any more we see how pretty it is."

Ada and I like to think that, in any event, the land has not passed to "outsiders." We believe that we are, by virtue not only of our ownership but also of our love and concern, as much a part of this land as anyone who traces his roots back to the days when Maine was simply a northern territory of Massachusetts. Right now, like every other landowner in the state—and, going a step further, like every other landowner in

America—we are confronted by a profound question: what is the best use for each piece of land? When the oilmen arrived in eastern Maine in 1968 this question became the ostensible point over which men and women passionately debated matters even closer to the core of their being.

*

PART·FIVE
The Dilemma

14 A
LIBERAL
EDUCATION

I 🌿 "THERE IS A COLOSSAL SHORTAGE of understanding about the oil industry," Robert T. Haslam, Vice-President of the Standard Oil Company of New Jersey (now the Exxon Corporation), told a meeting of the American Petroleum Institute in 1946. "We propose to increase that understanding. We propose to do it through a carefully planned series of specific steps that will create a constructive, favorable impression of the oil industry in the public mind. We want the public to like the oil industry."

That immediate postwar year, then, may be looked back on as something of a watershed in the history of the American oil industry's relationship with the public. The ensuing public-relations campaign has included those innocuous bits of televised hokum by which an oil company tries to convince people that its service-station attendants have sunnier dispositions, its rest rooms cleaner toilet bowls, and its gasoline more virility than those of its competitors. But the campaign has had other facets, whose aims are to muddle issues rather than to enhance

161

brand names. The industry needs to be . . . well, if not *loved*, at least admired and thought vital to the country's greatness. The old image of rapacious trusts implanted in the public mind by the first John D. Rockefeller has had to be expunged and replaced by that of a high-minded and adventurous group of men acting always in the nation's best interests.

By playing on this image the oilmen have been able to dampen the public outrage while using their power to extract an astonishing series of concessions and subsidies from the government. Wrapped securely in the cloak of patriotism, they ran roughshod over the public interest until a series of incidents that became environmental rallying cries—*Torrey Canyon*, Santa Barbara, and Machiasport—shed some long-diverted light on their industry's structure. Attention, of course, was turned on the oil industry chiefly *because* of those incidents. In few cases did the government agencies responsible for regulating the industry contribute their share of candlepower. Instead, the light originated with private citizens coming to grips for the first time with a phenomenon of extraordinary complexity.

Conservationists, in the past, have often been branded "crackpots" or "little old women in tennis shoes" because, in the face of some threat to their environment, their instincts were noble but their information meager. Faced in public hearings by industry's glib lawyers and spokesmen, the conservationists were easily confused. And so, when the specter of oil at Machiasport arose, there were those of us private citizens who made up our minds to learn what we could about the men and the industry we would deal with in debate. Continuing Education is a requirement for survival in the Age of Ecology.

"Most people conserve when there is too little," Harvey O'Connor observed in *The Empire of Oil*, "the oil industry conserves when there is too much."

It is an approach born of bitter past experience and it accounts for some of the wild contradictions within this schizophrenic industry. At times fears have been expressed that the United States is going to run out of oil reserves, thus exposing itself to the dubious mercy of foreign governments. But always, in the moment of despair, the earth has surrendered its gushers. Such a moment came in 1930 when an old wildcatter named Columbus M. (Dad) Joiner tapped an enormous oil field on the Widow Daisy Bradford's farm in East Texas. This discovery, added to new fields in other parts of the country, provided more oil than even the great refineries were able to handle, and certainly more oil than the public wanted to buy just as the Depression engulfed the country. The price of oil dropped from $1.30 to a nickel a barrel; a local saloon advertised beer at "ten cents a glass, or one barrel of oil." Beset by financial and legal problems, Dad Joiner sold his East Texas holdings to a professional gambler named H. L. Hunt, who survived the crisis to become one of the world's richest men.

Meanwhile, worried government officials, and finally the oil industry itself, tried to grapple with a peculiarity of the business that leads not only to waste and inefficiency, but also to overproduction and, ultimately, falling prices. An oil well extracts the flow at a single point above ground. The oil itself, however, lies at points underground that may be some distance laterally as well as horizontally from the property on which the well has been drilled. A well drilled on Farmer Brown's plot may be sucking up oil that is located in the rocks beneath the property of his neighbors, Smith and Jones, who have no legal grounds for complaint under the "law of capture." The only recourse open to Smith and Jones is to drill wells of their own and extract what they can before Brown takes the lion's share.

What happened in East Texas and at other rich oil fields where production was not controlled has been compared to the action of a group of children huddled over a single glass of soda. Each child thrusts his own straw into the soda, sucking frantically to capture his share before he loses it to the others.

If he works with two or three straws, so much the better for him. In the same way, the big western oil fields bristled with oil derricks as each Brown, Smith, and Jones sank wells cheek by jowl in a frantic race to get what they felt was their fair proportion of the black gold. In Kilgore, Texas, thirty-two wells were drilled in an area equal to a single city block. In other places the legs of derricks crisscrossed each other. Such runaway production techniques inevitably lead not only to a glut of oil but to inefficiency, too; the natural gases or underground water supplies that will help push oil to the surface in a gush under ordinary conditions are dissipated rapidly when wells are drilled willy-nilly, thus causing some of the oil to be lost, and the rest to be recovered eventually only by expensive pumping techniques.

Under pressure from conservation-minded federal and state officials, the oil industry eventually agreed to the regulation of production. The big oil-producing states established the rate ("prorationing") at which oil could be produced monthly from each well under its jurisdiction. The federal government (through the Connally Act of 1935) made it a crime to transport in interstate commerce oil that had been produced in violation of state regulations.

What does all this mean to the consumer in Chicago, Atlanta, Scarsdale, Brookline, or Bangor? It means, for one thing, higher prices, not simply because production is regulated but also because under the state's quota of withdrawals the most expensive oil is tapped first. The system is designed to give preference to the inefficient wells. The poorest wells sometimes are allowed to produce oil to the limit of their capacity, often by expensive pumping procedures, while the more productive wells that would give up their oil rapidly and in great quantity are legally restricted to only a small percentage of their potential. This inefficient and costly system might shake up our notions about the oil industry's close ties with the politicians unless we remember that large numbers of people (all of them presumably voters) own tiny shares in these inefficient "stripper" wells. The men who set the allowances are elected officials. It is unlikely that these officials would offend the shareholders (who vote them into office) by cutting the price of oil for consumers in distant states.

Oilmen are not reluctant to defend prorationing in their own words, citing the need to keep the little fellow in business, the need to keep ample oil reserves on hand in case of national emergencies, and the waste and inefficiency that would result should the states allow drillers to revert to the wild races of yesteryear. But more recently they prefer to quote from the report of a man reputed to be hostile to their interests. This is what a Justice Department report, signed by Attorney General Robert F. Kennedy, said in 1963:

By the late 1920's the waste of open flow production achieved status as a national problem. . . . Each new field discovery meant an intense competition to produce first and fastest, each producer seeking to get the oil above ground before he lost it to the adjacent producer. . . . Thus each new field was a repetition of waste in oil, pollution of water sources and extreme hazard of fire and explosion. . . . Besides valuable physical and economic waste the production race entailed even greater underground losses. Open flow production quickly destroyed the equilibrium of pressures in the reservoir and increased the viscosity of the oil. Fields so mishandled became quickly unproducible, leaving 85 to 90 per cent or more of the original oil in place, still untouched and unrecoverable. . . .

This escalated the local cycle of glut, waste, wide price swings and rapid depletion to the status of a serious national problem. . . . Rules requiring ratable take within a reservoir seem beyond question essential to end the gross waste in oil production which evoked the need for conservation. . . . Clearly this market control was not a surreptitious or illegal affair aimed at "fixing" prices at a particular level. Rather the States concerned were operating to support and stabilize crude oil markets and therefore prices in furtherance of the objectives of relevant Federal and State law. . . . The unleashing of the presently controlled supply could play havoc with the normal functioning of the industry and wipe out precisely those independent elements in refining and production which are now so important to competition.

If there are sound reasons for maintaining this crutch for prices (even here, many of the industry's critics are not entirely convinced that the system should be weighted to favor the most inefficient wells), some of the other regulations that aid the oilmen are patently less defensible. The notorious oil-depletion allowance is among them. This enormous tax advantage was devised with the income tax itself in 1913, when friendly Congressmen handed the operators of "extractive industries" such as mining and oil drilling their coveted exemptions. During the 1920s the allowance rose to 27.5 per cent. The basis for this allowance is the contention that oilmen have made sizable investments in wells which naturally decrease in value as they extract the oil. The oilmen then use the money saved on their depletion allowance to drill new wells, thus perpetuating the cycle. Meanwhile, other oilmen continue to claim the allowance though they have not sunk a well in years.

II 🌿 THE OIL-DEPLETION ALLOWANCE rankles taxpayers, but will remain a part of the American way until the public unites to overcome the pressures on Congress exerted by the nation's most powerful lobby. There was still another aspect of privilege that affected the public adversely, this time as consumers rather than as taxpayers. Like prorationing in American wells, the quota system on foreign oil pushed prices higher and kept them there. After years of debate, the controversial quota system was abolished by

President Nixon in 1973. Because it played a large part in what happened in the Maine oil dispute, its history deserves our attention.

American oilmen have been deeply involved in foreign oil fields for a long time. Working sometimes together and sometimes in cut-throat competition, the giants of the industry once were able to bully the governments of the nations from which they extracted oil, especially in Latin America and the Middle East. In fact, these giants work so closely when danger threatens that they have been called the "seven sisters." * After World War II the huge fields in the Middle East began to produce, under intensive drilling, enormous quantities of oil. Smaller, independent companies entered the picture, taking their share of Middle Eastern and, later, African oil. Much of this oil was shipped to Western Europe and Japan, both rebuilding their shattered economies after the war, but without oil resources of their own. Despite this demand, the United States remained the prime market. During the 1950s the shipment of foreign oil to this country in large quantities affected the industry very much, as had the glut of the early 1930s.

Oil from the Middle East, where labor is cheap and the oil fields rich, proved to be less expensive to produce than oil from America. Yet, as supplies poured in from abroad, the consequent surplus held down the price of American oil. The giants of the industry, since their supplies came from both sources, would have survived that state of affairs with little inconvenience, but the thousands of small producers who were restricted to their American holdings felt themselves jeopardized. No industry has ever had so many friendly ears to pour complaints into in Washington. Eisenhower's Republican administration was almost scandalously "soft" on the oilmen;

* The seven major oil companies, listed in the order of their size, are Exxon, Royal Dutch Shell, Mobil, Texaco, Gulf, Standard Oil of California, and British Petroleum. The last is, of course, British, while Royal Dutch Shell is controlled by both Dutch and British interests.

Senate Majority Leader Lyndon B. Johnson and Speaker of the House Sam Rayburn, both Democrats, were only too willing to placate, among their Texas constituents, the thousands of shareholders in American oil wells. Help came swiftly for the industry when, in 1959, the United States government instituted its quota system on oil imports.

Though the quota system was obviously an economic sop to the oil industry, its supporters in both parties justified it (and still do) on the basis of "national security." America must not become dependent on foreign sources of supply, so the reasoning goes; we must retain a healthy oil industry of our own to guard against those times when the undependable foreigners turn against us. Opponents of the oil-import quotas point out that if this is their basis it would be wiser in defense terms, as well as more economical for the American consumer, to set aside federal oil reserves for use in an emergency, meanwhile draining the cheaper foreign reserves as we conserve our own. Since the oilmen know that economics and not security is the unspoken point, the argument gets nowhere.

Here, in brief, is how the quota system worked. The Secretary of the Interior, acting on information supplied to him by the Oil Import Administration, set the quantity of foreign oil that could be imported to this country during each six-month period. The total averaged about 12.2 per cent of domestic production. Certain oil companies were allotted a percentage of this total as their import quota for the period, the companies and their quotas being determined by a complicated series of calculations that included the companies' "historic quotas," their refining capacity, and certain other indices.

After a decade the system became so riddled with "exemptions" and other contradictions that it came to bear no relation to a rational system. Companies that had no refineries of their own and no need for imports, and yet somehow had fallen beneficiaries to a set of the quota "tickets," peddled them at high prices to other companies. Those areas of the

country where refineries have not been built and whose
residents would benefit from low-cost foreign oil had to rely on
higher-priced oil shipped to them from the Southwest.

Consider Portland, Maine. Portland is second only to
Philadelphia as an oil port on the Atlantic Coast, receiving
shipments from both American ports in the Gulf of Mexico
and foreign sources. The oil from American wells is for use in
the state. Until recently the foreign oil could not be touched
because it was not covered by import quotas. Instead, the oil
(in greater quantities annually than is used in the entire state
of Maine) was transferred at Portland directly to a pipeline
which carried it 320 miles to Montreal. There it was sold to
Canadians at two or three cents a gallon *less* than New
Englanders paid for the oil shipped to them from the Gulf
ports.

Yet, under the quota system, one's proximity to a refinery
did not necessarily diminish the cost of one's gasoline and fuel
oil. Consider, this time, Hawaii. There Standard Oil of
California held the oil-import quota tickets for the islands,
thus controlling their imports, their only refinery and, of
course, the local prices. The oil itself is the world's cheapest,
taken from fields in the Middle East and Indonesia which
Standard owns in common with several of the industry's other
giants.

"Standard imports oil to Hawaii under its assigned quotas
and produces almost exactly as much gasoline as is sold in the
state," David Sanford reported in the *New Republic* (August 30,
1969). "It could meet all of Hawaii's needs for gasoline, and at
reasonable prices. But there is no competition and Standard
manipulates upward the price of gas. At the retail level,
estimates of overcharges to customers vary from $13 to $23
million a year—$39 to $69 for every motor vehicle in Hawaii."

The deepening energy crisis of 1973 put an end to the quota
system. If this were a simple world and oil a simple business,
the removal of oil-import quotas would solve most of our
problems. The discovery of a great field on Alaska's North

Slope, the unimaginably huge potential for extracting oil from the shale deposits in our Western states, and even the still-considerable normal reserves elsewhere in those states, constitute a mineral resource that could be set aside and developed by the federal government for national emergencies. Even the politicians who are most entangled with the oilmen know that to use "national security" as a justification for import quotas was a sham; the quotas were operable simply because they were economically desirable for a comparatively small group of people. But the politics and economics of the oil industry go on endlessly creating their own mysterious obstacles to the free flow of supplies.

III ❧ THERE IS STILL ANOTHER complication to the unrestricted shipment of oil over long distances. That is the environmental hazard which, until quite recently, was muted by industry and government alike. Oil has always been a pollutant, of course; tankers broke up or deliberately pumped out their oily wastes at sea, while human and mechanical failures during the transfer of cargoes caused spills of varying size in port. But the world's oceans are vast, and the spills were comparatively small. "It rains into the sea, and still the sea is salt," A. E. Housman wrote; what further impact could man make upon it with all his piddling works? Even the frequent destruction of tankers by submarines during World War II seldom caused serious pollution problems. All too often the torpedoes set off intense fires which consumed the oil, while the aviation fuel that escaped from sinking tankers was quickly volatilized.

Geared to war production, American shipyards not only kept pace with the destruction at sea, but eventually built a fleet of tankers equal to the entire world's prewar total. Many of these replacements were the new T2 tankers, at 16,500 deadweight tons, substantially larger than their predecessors. The trend toward larger tankers had, in fact, begun as oil soon accounted for more than half of the world's trade by sea. The demand for oil rose after the war with unforeseen rapidity, not simply to satisfy the increasing size and number of internal-combustion engines, industrial machines, and home heating plants, but also for its by-products. The revolution in technology was under way. Oil-based chemicals, composed chiefly of carbon and hydrogen compounds, that the industry once considered "waste" from the refining process now were sold to be used in the manufacture of an incredibly diverse range of products. Plastics, fertilizers (from petroleum-based ammonia), detergents, pesticides (including DDT), nylon and other synthetic fibers, and even TNT, were among the goods produced by the flourishing petrochemical industry.

Thus great new industrial complexes grew up around oil refineries. They provided jobs, but they also polluted and devastated their environs. Despite the oil industry's glossy advertising campaign to persuade the dazzled public that oil refineries "make good neighbors," the truth is that eventually only slums are able to coexist with them; not many refinery executives take up residence next door to their place of business.

But the desolation that usually surrounds a refinery and a petrochemical complex is only the first circle of our modern industrial hell. As Barry Commoner has pointed out in *The Closing Circle*,* it was this technological revolution that is primarily responsible for our present environmental disaster. The natural products—wood, glass, animal and vegetable fats—that once were the basis of our manufactured goods were easily recycled or broken down rather quickly in the open environment. Their replacements, such as many of the petroleum-based components of plastics, detergents, pesticides, and

* Alfred A. Knopf, New York, 1971.

synthetic fibers, persist almost indefinitely, poisoning or at best simply cluttering the world we live in.

Among the most persistent and omnipresent of these pollutants is oil itself. In Japan, Italy, and elsewhere giant tankers began to emerge from the shipyards, ordered by the oilmen in Texas, New York, London, and the other centers of the industry who had seen the enormous potential in savings that these ships represented. Once tankers surpass 35,000 tons, they are so efficient that the costs for crew, accommodations, and maintenance rise only insignificantly in proportion to their bulk. It is said that the oil companies save nearly a penny on each gallon they ship in a supertanker.

If one does a few simple calculations, the extent of that saving is apparent. Using as an example one of the new 312,000 DWT * tankers, we find that it is capable of carrying 2,250,000 barrels of oil. A barrel contains 42 gallons. Thus the savings on a single shipment theoretically approach a million dollars. Balancing the savings are a shortage of deep-water harbors able to accept these giants, the expensive shore facilities needed to hold the discharged cargoes, and the specter of a maritime disaster. Someone has estimated that, in the event a 312,000-ton tanker breaks up, it has the potential to coat each foot along a 200-mile shoreline with two barrels of crude oil.

The public remained blissfully unaware of this potential until the *Torrey Canyon* broke up on a Cornish rock. Although small compared to some of the ships now coming out of the Japanese shipyards, the *Torrey Canyon* was manifestly a supertanker, measuring 974 feet 5 inches long, drawing 54 feet, and carrying 117,000 deadweight tons. During the middle 1960s she and a sister ship were the longest merchant vessels in the world.

At the time of the disaster there was much confusion about

* Deadweight tons. This refers to a ship's carrying capacity. Deadweight tonnage is measured in long tons, 2240 pounds each. It is the total weight, including cargo, stores, fuel, and even crew and passengers, that will bring a ship to its legal waterline.

who owned the *Torrey Canyon*, and no wonder! The men who ship the oil dislike the idea of using vessels registered under the United States flag because of the high costs. Foreign ships and crews represent an important saving. By law, only United States ships may carry cargo between two United States ports, as, for instance, between the Gulf states and New England. But anything goes in international trade. American ship-owners find it to their advantage to register their ships in the international trade under "flags of convenience," specifically the happily pliant governments of Liberia, Panama, and Honduras, in order to evade United States taxes and labor unions.

In his excellent book, *Oil and Water: The Torrey Canyon*,* Edward Cowan shows that the ship was owned by the Barracuda Tanker Corporation, whose "head office is a filing cabinet in Hamilton, Bermuda, although it is incorporated in Monrovia, Liberia." This corporation was created by Dillon Read and Company, an investment-banking house on Wall Street, "to accommodate its good client, Union Oil Company." Barracuda then leased the ship to Union Oil, because under United States tax laws it is cheaper for an oil company to lease a ship than to own one.

"The *Torrey Canyon*," Cowan writes, "was the property of a company owned by Americans, incorporated in Liberia and nominally doing business in Bermuda, a British colony. Under long-term charter to Union Oil Company of California, the ship was manned by an Italian crew and on her fatal voyage was on single-voyage charter to British Petroleum, which is 49 per cent owned by the British government."

All the world knows the story of the *Torrey Canyon*'s fate: how, on the morning of March 18, 1967, the vessel's captain, racing to reach Milford Haven on high tide and save precious time, chose a treacherous passage through the reefs around the Scilly Islands off England's southwest coast; and how, part

* Lippincott, New York, 1968.

way through that passage, the *Torrey Canyon*'s bottom was ripped open as it went aground on a submerged rock. Much of its thirty-five million gallons of Kuwait crude oil drifted away, killing sea birds, fish, and other marine organisms and fouling some of the most heavily used resort beaches along the English and French coasts.

The *Torrey Canyon*'s fate first of all awakened millions of people to the fact that tankers of this size (and even twice its size) were sailing the world's oceans. Moreover, it became apparent that safety regulations for oil transport were appallingly weak. In the event of a disaster there was no technology to deal with spills of the magnitude inevitable with supertankers, while there was great difficulty in affixing liability under the maze of ownerships, registrations, and charters that surrounded their operation. (In 1969, Union Oil Company and Barracuda agreed to pay damages of $7.2 million toward a final cleanup.)

The whole issue of oil pollution, barely recognized before, had suddenly taken on enormous complications. Economies of scale were pushing the oil companies in the direction of transport by supertanker; the "Six-Day" Arab-Israeli War of 1967, which led to the shutdown of the Suez Canal, increased the need for more supertankers to carry oil from the Middle East the long way around the Cape of Good Hope to Western markets.

And then, in the wake of the *Torrey Canyon*, the press reported an epidemic of other mishaps at sea—tankers breaking up, or accidently fouling the surrounding water during loading or refueling. From around the world there came reports that the sea was sickening under its mounting burden of oil. Fisheries experts revealed that pollution, mainly from oil, had sharply decreased the diversity of fishes in the Mediterranean. Thor Heyerdahl announced that, while he drifted across the Atlantic on *Ra II*, he and his crew sometimes found the ocean so filthy they could not use its water to wash their clothes. Other scientists discovered that the chemicals they had added to oil spills in an attempt to control them proved more lethal to marine organisms than the oil itself.

"Imagine how clever of mankind," Jacques Cousteau remarked, "when he has a big slick of poison on top of the water, to add something to it that will make it sink slowly and kill everything in its path, all the way to the bottom."

Less than two years after the *Torrey Canyon* struck a Cornish reef the United States suffered a major oil disaster of its own. In January 1969 a leak in a well drilled off the California coast covered four hundred square miles with oil and fouled forty miles of shoreline along the Santa Barbara Channel. Millions of Americans watched the devastation unfold on their television screens. Dying birds, slimed beaches, and outraged citizens all etched their images in the national consciousness. Oil, once firmly equated with wealth in that consciousness, suddenly seemed, for the mass of people, more likely to be a harbinger of desolation.

What had really happened was that, for the first time, large numbers of Americans were beginning to realize that economic issues did not absolutely dictate the kind of environment in which they must live. Perhaps, if they chose, they could say no to oil or any other man-made peril to the world around them. Perhaps, after all, there were choices to be made.

15

THE 300,000-TON
PANACEA

IN SEPTEMBER 1967 Senator Muskie wrote a letter to
his friend, Secretary of the Interior Stewart L.
Udall. It said, in part: "Jack Evans is delivering this letter,
together with a letter from Governor Curtis and a memoran-
dum outlining a proposal for a deepwater port and industrial
complex in the area of Machias, Maine. . . . I hope it will be
possible for the Department to use the authority available to it
to permit the location of such a facility in the continental
United States."

John K. Evans, the man for whom Muskie had written the
letter as an introduction to Udall, was a former oil-industry
executive who had been working for some years with prominent officials of Maine's government to locate a large refinery
in the state. There was a thorny legal obstacle to fulfilling
Evans' dream. This obstacle was the complicated system of
import quotas that had been established by the federal
government in 1959 and that tended to keep domestic oil
prices high. The price of oil is a critical problem in New

England, which has no indigenous supply of coal or oil, yet is dependent on great quantities of fuel because it is a manufacturing center and its winter climate is extremely cold; New England's per-capita consumption of heating oil is three and a half times that of the national average.

There were other reasons for Muskie, who was, I believe, genuinely concerned about Maine's welfare, to go along with Evans' scheme to build a terminal and refinery in eastern Maine. The federal Economic Development Administration had already designated Washington County a "depressed area." Furthermore, as the leader of the antipollution brigade in the Senate, Muskie was interested in the possibility that low-sulfur crude oil would be imported to the proposed refinery, and thus help to alleviate air pollution in the cities.

The plan devised by Muskie, Evans, and Maine's Governor Kenneth M. Curtis included several steps. The first was to get the Department of Commerce to declare a free-trade subzone at Machiasport. Under federal law, certain restricted areas of the country may be designated exempt from many import barriers, permitting importers to bring raw materials into the zone without having to pay customs duties on them. Such exemptions permit the importers to process or refine the materials, then ship the finished products out again to overseas markets, or sell them in the United States; in the latter case, import duties must be paid when the products pass out of the free-trade zone into the American market. During the Johnson administration, oil was put into a separate category, with dealers needing a permit from the Secretary of the Interior if it was to be among the raw materials brought to a free port.

Muskie and the others felt that the basic conditions already existed for carrying out their plan. Off Machiasport was the depth of water (one hundred feet and more) needed to accommodate the supertankers that would make the shipment of oil to a refinery there economically desirable. Several oil companies became genuinely interested in the plan, including the Occidental Petroleum Corporation. Occidental's interest was stimulated by the discovery of a rich oil field to which it had access in Libya. The most profitable markets for this low-sulfur oil would be in America, but Occidental had no import quotas under which to ship it here. By riding on the coattails of Maine's interested politicians, Occidental hoped to solve the problem of what to do with its Libyan oil.

Under the plan, Occidental was to build a giant terminal and refinery at Machiasport. The state of Maine applied to the Department of Commerce to designate Portland a free-trade zone (so that it would be able to import a variety of products duty-free) and Machiasport a subzone for oil imports, which in turn required a license from the Interior Department. Occidental planned to refine 300,000 barrels of crude oil a day at its refinery. It would trans-ship part of the refined oil to other American and foreign ports in smaller tankers, and make the rest available as fuel oil and gasoline to New England. It was for this purpose that Occidental needed import quotas. The scheme's proponents thought it just a matter of time before a great petrochemical complex grew up around the refinery. Jobs and cheap fuel, it was said, would accrue to local residents.

Senator Muskie and Governor Curtis led the cheering section, which found echoes in the other New England states. The area's United States Senators closed ranks to support the proposal, applauding the benefits noted above and attacking the "distortions" spread by the late Representative Hale Boggs of Louisiana and other members of Congressional delegations from the oil-producing states in the South and West. The oil industry, in its turn, bitterly opposed any relaxation of the import quotas. The giant corporations which held quotas wanted no diminution of their monopoly status, while the smaller companies feared a deluge of foreign oil. Congressman Boggs publicly accused Occidental of sending emissaries to his office with a "bribe" in the form of a promise to finance his election campaign in exchange for his support of their position in Congress.

Reading the enthusiastic projections about a refinery's benefits, some of us in Washington County grew uneasy. For instance, in challenging the inflated claims of the Westerners about the quota system's importance to national security, the New England Senators produced some disquieting notions of their own.

"Proponents of our current oil policies maintain that the import control program, coupled with the oil depletion allowance, encourages domestic oil exploration, which in turn contributes significantly to our national security," the Senators said. "What the proponents fail to mention is that the current oil-import regulations have forced the concentration of well over a third of our total refinery capacity in the Texas-Louisiana Gulf area. These Gulf refineries are likely to become the vulnerable first targets of an attacking enemy."

It seemed to be the Senators' aggregate position that the bombs should be spread around, so that Down Easters received their fair share. And besides, in all of the early proposals there were no specific plans for pollution control, no hint that the best use of a lovely peninsula such as that below Machiasport might be as something other than the site of a huge refinery and petrochemical complex.

With just such fanfare, technological man has introduced each new manifestation of material progress during the twentieth century. Whether he was about to spread DDT through the world ecosystem, or deliver that mobile pollution machine—a new automobile—to a prospective buyer, this incurable optimist has aimed only for an immediate economic impact. Broader questions, even if they occurred to him, were dismissed as irrelevant. The experts, as usual, would try to solve an economic problem by putting people to work destroying the environment.

The official position apparently was summed up by Jack Evans, as quoted in a Portland newspaper. "You couldn't do this in Casco Bay because you might spoil beaches," Evans said of the more populated, tourist-oriented area along the western part of the Maine coast. "In Machiasport there are no beaches, no cross currents, no hazards."

It was left to private citizens in the area to question this description of their surroundings. One of them was Charles Dorchester, a graduate of the Yale Divinity School and a Methodist minister with three small churches in eastern Maine. Dorchester's hobby is bird watching. A visitor to the roomy house on a tree-shaded street in Machias where Dorchester lives with his wife and their two young sons will notice that the living room is dominated not by the expected religious articles but by a nineteenth-century collection of mounted birds. As he makes the rounds of his churches and youth groups, Dorchester keeps a pair of World War II binoculars beside him on the front seat of his secondhand station wagon in case he passes an interesting hawk or a flock of winter finches along the road. His only luxury is his camera equipment. Early in the morning, when the light is right, Dorchester will carry his equipment to a nearby marsh or the rocky shore to photograph herons, plovers, and curlews. It is his long-nursed ambition to make a film illustrating the life cycle of the chestnut-sided warbler; he believes it will not be a serious problem to photograph the bird on its breeding grounds in Maine, but he hasn't yet figured out the financing to allow him to follow it to its winter quarters in Central America.

Dorchester wondered what would be the effect of an oil industry on this part of the coast. Someone told him about my interest in the environment, and he called to ask me if I would attend a meeting with half a dozen other people at his house to talk about the prospect of oil at Machiasport. We gathered there one summer evening in 1968, coming to the conclusion, after several hours of talk, that all we were sure about was that the project made us uneasy. We decided to find out what we could about it. But, even if we collected some facts that justified our uneasiness, was there anything we could do to alter the plans that already had been set in motion? We were a handful of private citizens, while the state administration, the Congressional delegation, several interested oil companies, and the local boosters were solidly behind the project. Charles Dorchester said that he had taken a poll of the congregation at one of his churches on the previous Sunday, and sixty of the sixty-two people who responded to it favored oil at Machiasport.

We began to collect information on what an oil terminal and refinery had meant to other places. Meanwhile, we found that many more people than we had supposed seemed to share our concern. One of them was Gardiner Means, the well-known economist who had served in Franklin D. Roosevelt's brain trust and who owned an island in Machias Bay. He added "prestige" to our little group, as well as some valuable facts and a pipeline (if you will pardon the expression) to the seats of power. Dorchester organized an open meeting at Machias High School late that summer. At his request, both the Governor and the engineering firm for the most active of the oil companies, Occidental, sent representatives to answer the local people's questions. We had scheduled the meeting to begin at 7:30 in the evening. But by the time I arrived, at 6:45, it was already apparent that the small area we had cordoned off in one corner of the school cafeteria would not contain the crowd. We shifted chairs and rearranged our space, but still the people flowed in. Finally we moved in a body to the gymnasium across the yard, which fortunately proved to be one of the few halls in the area that could have accommodated the six hundred people who came to the meeting. It was an extraordinary crowd to assemble for any event other than a basketball game in our part of Maine.

Interest obviously ran high, but even at that early date there were indications of official confusion that raised doubts in the minds of the audience. What would be the impact on the area of the inevitable sudden population explosion accompanying a major construction project? No one seemed to know. Several residents, masters of ocean-going ships, raised the question of fogs, storms, and tides at Machiasport, all of which were locally known to be formidable. Apparently no thorough hydrologic studies had been made.

"Machiasport is a port in name only," one experienced seaman told the crowd. "Where you're planning to tie up these big tankers it's really only an open roadstead."

The plan, we learned, was to build the terminal on Stone Island, near the tip of the peninsula below Machiasport. After it was unloaded from the supertankers, the oil would be piped to a large refinery on the peninsula. The Governor's representative assured the audience that the refinery would not become an "eyesore" because trees would be planted around it. The people laughed.

No one asked harder questions than Gardiner Means. Why does the refinery have to be built right on the unique coastline, when there is plenty of available space for it only a few miles inland? Have pollution controls been written into the agreement between the state and the interested oil company?

The answer to the first question, as expressed by the Governor's representative, was that it would be impractical to pipe the oil inland from the terminal. ("Under the circumstances," countered economist Means, his calculations in hand, "the company's profits will be enormous. It can easily afford to build and maintain such a pipeline. All its other costs will be lower, including the cost of land, if it locates inland.") The answer to the second question, not really divulged until a later date, was no. In their haste to grab the brass ring presented by the prospect of oil, state officials had not got around to guarding against the effects of the inevitable spills and discharges.

It was a long evening. After several hours had passed, someone suggested from the floor that a poll be taken among those present to sample local feeling. The Governor's representative suggested that the poll be delayed until the end of the meeting. Then he launched into an interminable filibuster that drove most of the weary audience out of the building and

effectively precluded an opportunity for a poll. But the
meeting had established the necessity to prod the project's
supporters, in and out of government, into taking the environment into their calculations. It also had created a large body
of concerned residents.

Charles Dorchester's group was one of many local organizations that have sprung up locally along the coast, from
Eastport ("Save What's Left") to Portland ("Citizens Who
Care") to meet the threat of oil. Not the least of these groups'
problems has been to estimate in each case the validity of the
threat. In few cases has the foray been led by one of the oil
industry's giants. For the most part the "interested" companies
and promoters have been adventurers operating on flimsy
capital, buccaneers who looked on the Maine coast as simply
another underdeveloped country to be plucked, or globe-trot-
ting Micawbers who wandered in hoping that something
would turn up.

"When you look closely at one of these promoters," says
James Russell Wiggins, a former United States Ambassador to
the United Nations and a resident of eastern Maine, "you
usually find that what you've got is another guy looking for a
hunting license. A lot of them simply don't have the capital to
build a modern oil terminal or refinery. What they're looking
for is a finder's fee—they're hoping to set up the deal for
somebody else, and then sell out. It's called 'breaking the
coast.' "

The most publicized of the would-be oilmen at Machiasport
was Robert A. Gardner Monks. A graduate of Harvard
College and Harvard Law School, Monks is tall, athletic (he
was an oarsman at Harvard), and attractive enough so that I
once overheard a group of women from the Sierra Club, for
godssake, cooing over "that divine man." He was in his middle
thirties when Machiasport became a newspaper dateline. His
family had owned Roque Island nearby for many years.
"Divine" is an adjective that might very well be applied to
Roque Island—a darkly wooded crescent tapering to a beach

of pure whiteness on its inner side, delicately shaping one of the finest little harbors in eastern Maine. I remember cruising into that haven one afternoon when a thick fog descended on the Bay of Fundy as a friend and I were on our way to Grand Manan. Ketches and other small yachts were anchored in the harbor, waiting out the fog. At night a half-moon, "bright as a dollar," my friend said, burned through the fog overhead, while all around us the wisps of fog curled into an opaque curtain. When I saw the island in the next morning's clear dawn I understood why, by his own admission, the rest of Robert Monks's family refused to speak to the young man who was trying to set an oil terminal and a refinery into that landscape.

Monks had started his career with a prominent Boston law firm, but his marriage to Millicent Sprague, the daughter of the owner of C. H. Sprague and Son, a coal and oil distributor, altered his course. He eventually bought out his father-in-law's interest in the Sprague Company. When he learned that several oilmen were interested in developing Stone Island and the neighboring shore at Machiasport, Monks secured options on the island and key pieces of nearby land, acting, it is said, out of spite because he believed himself to have been snubbed by one of the interested oilmen, Dr. Armand Hammer of Occidental Petroleum Corporation. Monks created a new company, Atlantic World Port, Inc., with the stated intention of seeing that a terminal and refinery were built at Machiasport. It was a company whose only physical assets seemed to be Monks's options. Nevertheless, Monks stole the thunder from both Hammer of Occidental and Atlantic-Richfield, which also began exploring Machiasport's potential.

Meanwhile, the state was in the business of promoting an oil refinery, preferably buttressed by a petrochemical complex, in Washington County. The agency in charge of smoothing the way for the oil industry was the Department of Economic Development (whose initials, DED, sometimes prompt bemused observers at Augusta to refer to it as the Department of the Emotionally Disturbed). While the state's leaders spoke of "creative conservation," they had committed themselves to an enormous disturbance of the coast before any adequate studies had been made of its possible impact there.

Of course, Maine is not alone in falling victim to this development syndrome. Its occasional confusion of aim, however, is often made glaringly apparent because its leaders include such obviously well-intentioned men as Senator Muskie and Governor Curtis. Both, at the outset, were stanch supporters of the proposal to bring oil to Machiasport, and both argued in what may seem to be the best tradition of the most venerable wing of the conservation movement itself: that conservation is the wise use of our natural resources for the economic benefit of the most people.

—

This view became particularly attractive to state officials as they first came to grips with local economic conditions back in the 1950s. Senator Muskie has described these beginnings:

When I was elected governor in 1954 the major substantive issue was economic development. Maine had been plagued by slow growth, fits of isolated prosperity, and regional declines for almost one hundred years. The coastal counties, east of Sagadohac County, were suffering the worst deprivation. Economic development has been a major goal of every state administration since my first term as governor.

Governor Curtis spoke in a similar vein about his earlier experience with the Area Redevelopment Administration:

We had to get industry in then to get jobs for Maine people. We were quite successful. I think Maine now has an underemployment problem, not unemployment. What we have to do is shift our emphasis more to getting the right kind of industry for Maine. Then, when we raise the standard of Maine living as high as the standard enjoyed by most Americans, we can concentrate on the preservation of our fine environment.

As some states have already learned, those words might supply a fitting epitaph for their own once-fine environments. Even Senator Muskie saw the struggle during the early days at Machiasport as a "product of competing interests in land and water. Workmen out of jobs or locked in low-paying jobs want industrial growth for new opportunity. Summer residents and visitors and suburban residents want to limit industrial growth as a protection against interference in their own life styles." But what scientists and conservationists were beginning to say, as loudly and as urgently as they could, was that pollution control was no longer a matter of "life styles." It was a matter of survival.

The Governor released a set of statistics for Washington County that seemed to support his position on Machiasport:

> The per capita annual personal income is $2160, which is $450 below the State average, $900 below the national average and $1200 below the New England average. The 1969 unemployment rate in the county was 12.9 per cent compared with a State average of 4.6 per cent and a national average of 4.1 per cent.

These are stunning figures, and if they drew an accurate portrait of the county they might justify the sort of headlong approach to the problem that the state adopted. But, as we shall see, they do not tell the story. It was this misunderstanding, however, that prompted the haste by public figures to climb aboard the Machiasport bandwagon during the summer of 1968. Senator Muskie, to be sure, mentioned pollution control in his endorsement of the proposal, but he referred mainly to the nature of the imported oil itself, and not to the process of transporting or refining it:

> I support any legitimate move to produce low-sulfur, nonpolluting residual fuel oil, oil not presently being produced in this country. That is one reason I support the refinery at Machiasport which will produce such an oil because it will be refining low-sulfur crude oil from the Middle East.

But the first real steps toward protecting the coast in Washington County came about as a result of the persistent questioning by Charles Dorchester's group. In fact, the Governor withdrew some of the group's sting by selecting the prestigious Gardiner Means to be chairman of a newly created pollution-control subcommittee dealing with the Machiasport project. Under Dr. Means's guidance, the subcommittee persuaded the Governor to support the concept of building a refinery inland. It was further agreed that pollution controls would be written into agreements between the state and any oil companies that chose to locate in the Machiasport area.

As "earth days" and environmental fever swept across the country, men in high places conceded that in their zeal for economic development they must pay at least lip service to the concept of a livable world. That was surely a beginning.

16
THE POLITICS OF PRESERVATION

I ❧ IRONICALLY, the most formidable obstacle to rapid oil development came not from anyone who had the slightest concern for the Maine coast but from the oil industry itself.

Monks, holding his options close to his breast, waited for others to move. Hammer of Occidental had the oil and the plans. He controlled the flow of oil from Libya, where an important strike had recently been made, so that he sat uneasily on great quantities of the low-sulfur oil that had excited Senator Muskie's interest but which Hammer could not import to the United States because of the quota system. His plan to build a large refinery at Machiasport to refine 300,000 barrels a day depended on the politicians' success in getting the necessary approval for a foreign-trade zone and a relaxation of federal quotas.

The giants of the oil industry, jealous of what they considered to be the prospect of special concessions to Occidental, pleaded with the federal government to continue holding the protective blanket of oil regulation over their threatened heads; irresoluteness, they warned, would undermine the nation's security by making it dependent on foreign oil. In his book, *The Politics of Ecology*, James Ridgeway has put the situation in a clearer perspective:

> At base, the system depends on making sure there is impetus to drill for oil within the continental United States. A high rate of U.S. production is absolutely necessary for establishing a big tax write-off, which, in turn, is essential in maximizing profits.

In any case, the orthodox oilmen challenged Occidental's claims that a refinery at Machiasport would reduce New England's fuel prices. Fuel prices there were high, they admitted, but they claimed that this was due mainly to high markups by retailers in that region, rather than to exorbitant wholesale prices. A Mobil Oil Corporation spokesman went further:

> While Occidental's avowed pricing policy is purportedly aimed at reducing costs to the consumer, we believe this claim is spurious. Price reductions, if offered initially, would be only at the refinery level. There is no evidence or assurance that they would be passed on to the consumers. If they were, however, the viability of competing marketers, as well as refiners, would be adversely affected.

There may have been a generous ration of sour grapes in all this, but in any case conservationists gained time to make a closer analysis of the claims that had been advanced by the project's proponents. No one claimed that the Maine coast was virgin territory for oil. Portland, as we have seen, has been for a long time one of the major oil ports on the East Coast, handling almost 600,000 barrels a day. But oil comes to Portland, as well as to a number of smaller Maine ports, in conventional tankers and barges, and the state has suffered its share of the spills that are an inevitable part of the business of moving oil. But now the industry is changing. Just as the great trailer trucks that overwhelm our network of highways proliferate because they cut transportation costs, so the oil industry is turning increasingly to supertankers. A supertanker's psychological impact cannot be measured simply in orders of magnitude; it becomes, in the public mind, a whole new species of monster. Maine's fishermen, summer visitors, and a great variety of other residents responded with an involuntary shudder to the specter of a new *Torrey Canyon* breaking up along the coast.

The reluctance of the oil and shipping industries to assume responsibility for a catastrophe did nothing to relieve anxiety. When shipping executives appeared before Senator Muskie's Subcommittee on Air and Water Pollution, they opposed legislation that would force them to pay the cost of cleaning up accidental spills, claiming it would be "an intolerable burden." Ralph E. Casey of the American Institute of Merchant Shipping wanted a strictly limited liability for shippers.

"Who should pay the cost above that?" Muskie wanted to know.

"Well, perhaps the government," Casey ventured, adding that it would be money well spent because it would keep the United States Merchant Marine alive.

Local groups along the coast found active support for their position in the Natural Resources Council of Maine, which is based in Augusta. The Council served as a rallying point for accumulating both funds and information. It was instrumental in organizing a group that is not tax-exempt, the Coastal Resources Action Committee (CRAC), one of whose purposes is to hire two lobbyists to present the conservationists' position in the state legislature. Most conservation organizations cannot engage in active lobbying because it would place in jeopardy their special status, which allows that contributions from private citizens may be deducted from the donors' income tax. Funds channeled through the CRAC gave conservationists a chance to make their wishes known in an arena that had always been dominated by the spokesmen for Maine's industries.

With progress toward building a refinery bogged down in the national dispute over oil quotas, the conservationists pushed two important bills through the legislature in the winter of 1969–1970. One, the "Oil Conveyance Act," imposes a levy of half a cent a barrel on oil products passing either way between terminals and vessels. The funds realized from this levy are to be used to compensate victims of spills for whatever damages they have suffered and to carry out surveillance and research programs.

The other bill, passed as the "Site Selection Act," authorizes the state's Environmental Improvement Commission to approve or disapprove a site selected by the industry for major installations such as terminals, tank farms, or refineries. Theoretically, the Commission may finally disapprove as too hazardous, or as incompatible with the area's development, an oil project such as the one proposed at Machiasport. As Donaldson Koons, the chairman of the Commission said, "The state is just beginning to realize there are some industries it cannot *afford* to have here." In the wake of this legislation, there were exclamations of relief (both from inside and outside the state) that even if the oil industry gained a foothold on the coast, Maine now had the means to alleviate the potential residue of destruction. It was not so; as if to prove the conservationists' contention that the oil industry would not act in good faith, the industry went to court to challenge the validity of Maine's protective legislation.

Elsewhere, to the south, I have walked along stretches of coast where the oil traffic was heavy. If I went barefoot, the oil stuck to the soles of my feet in flattened clots, and it was simpler to wash afterward with kerosene than with soap and water. The oil that covered the rocks along the way might cling there for years. I have seen birds that were trapped in slicks offshore, preening their plumage incessantly (and thus poisoning themselves) to try to rub off the congealed oil that transformed each feather from an airy complexity to a sticky lump, useless alike for insulation and flight. Volunteers worked for hours to clean their feathers, but in the end nearly all of the birds died.

The stretch of coast on which Machiasport lies has an almost infinite variety of natural treasures, whether one approaches it by land or sea. Its rocky shore, its islands, its seals and its birds, its lobsters and its clam flats defy even an oil corporation's economist to put a price tag on them. Among the living things most vulnerable to oil are the birds of the seagoing family called alcids—auks, murres, dovekies, guillemots, and puffins. Machias Seal Island, lying ten miles off this stretch of coastline, is the site of the largest breeding colony of puffins along the eastern coast of the United States.

Ada and I have had a proprietary feeling about that island for a long time. Nearly every summer we try to spend at least a day there in the midst of the bustling puffinry. One year we took with us the twin sons of a local lobster fisherman to spend a week living with a lighthouse keeper and his wife on the island and gathering the background for a children's book that we later wrote called *Puffin Island*.* The confusion over Machias Seal Island's ownership is symbolic, I think, of the common interest linking the United States and Canada in this part of the world. This fourteen-acre island of rock and turf seemed to have been assigned to the United States by treaty after the War of 1812, but its remoteness in a world of formidable tides, currents, and fogs hardly made it a desirable place for settlement. Its only significance seemed to be as a marine landmark on pleasant days and a hazard on ugly ones. In 1832, after a number of their ships had pounded themselves to pieces on the island's rocky sides, the merchants of St. John, New Brunswick, levied a shipping tax on themselves to provide the money to build a lighthouse there. The island was, in effect, seized by a foreign power, though the United States did not trouble itself to protest.

* Cowles, New York, 1971.

Before writing about the island I wanted to determine its ownership. A man of affairs had once told me that if one wants a prompt reply to a question from the United States Government, one should neither write nor telephone, but rather send a telegram. I wired Dean Rusk, then Secretary of State and up to his ears in Vietnam, about Machias Seal Island's status. I imagine that the question must have seemed somewhat irrelevant to the Secretary at that troublesome time, and that his first impulse might have been to tell an aide to find out where the hell it was and bomb it. But whatever the sequence of events, my wire filtered down through a succession of underlings until it found a place on the desk of the Director for Relations with Canada, who enlightened me thus:

According to United States Hydrographic office publication No. 30, "List of Lights and Fog Signals," Volume 1, January 1, 1955, the Canadian Government maintains a lighthouse and a fog signal on Machias Seal Island. Nevertheless, the presence of these navigational stations on the island does not imply Canadian sovereignty. The matter of ownership has never been finalized by the United States Government and the Government of Canda.

In any case, the puffins are an ornament to our part of the world. These "sea parrots" with their grotesque ridged bills, wagon-red and triangular, and neat black-and-white plumage, appear to have stepped freshly from the illuminated pages of some fanciful medieval bestiary. It is an endless delight to sit in a blind in the puffinry and watch them at close range. Smaller than gulls, they lounge on the rocks like shiftless little men in formal dress, sometimes huddling in groups, at other times bustling over to investigate a minor commotion among their neighbors. Occasionally one waddles to an opening in the rocks, which is its nesting burrow, and disappears. The flying birds, returning from the sea with food for their young, introduce a further fanciful note. Slender silver fish, drooping from both sides of the great bill like gleaming mustaches, pose the inevitable question: How does the puffin, with five little fishes in its bill, capture a sixth without losing all the rest? No one seems to be certain.

A matter that scientists know a little more about is the puffin's susceptibility to oil. "A poet is a penguin," E. E. Cummings said, "his wings are to swim with." So are a puffin's short stubby wings, constructed like paddles that propel the bird underwater in pursuit of fish. (Many other families of aquatic birds, including ducks, propel themselves underwater with their feet.) Outside of the breeding season, when it is flying back and forth between the water and its burrow, the puffin spends most of its time on the water's surface. There it is especially vulnerable to the oil slicks that cover so much of the sea today, and there are stories of great slicks slowly enveloping the puffins, as ice traps an unwary duck that has dozed off on a pond on a freezing night. The puffin's population apparently is declining in the North Atlantic. It is disquieting to remember that man finished off the puffin's close relative, the great auk, with cleaner weapons a century ago.

And so I was thinking of puffins, among other sublime things, when the oilmen began to probe the Maine coast. Are puffins a trivial consideration? I can't believe that anyone who has ever seen a puffin would think so. But are puffins trivial in relation to people and their problems? I believe that that is a stupid question, and I repeat it here only because it is the sort of intimidating diversion the exploiters create when they come up against arguments that cannot be answered by a glance at their bookkeeper's ledger. ("Are you for birds or people?" asks the pesticide salesman when another chemically induced outrage is brought to his attention.) Must we choose? A lot of us happen to believe that an island or an ocean or a world that is good for puffins is good for people, too, and that an oil-soaked puffin is a discouraging portent for all the other species with which it shares the earth.

With a lot of other people, I jumped into the Machiasport controversy. I attended meetings and contributed money and wrote letters to politicians and newspapers. I could fight in a professional capacity, too, writing an article for *Audubon* and helping the Natural Resources Council of Maine to produce a booklet of questions and answers about oil and the Maine coast. There are a lot of good people who approach a controversy such as this having swallowed the exploiters' contention that we must choose—between people and puffins, or fish, or clean water, or even an uncontaminated environment. (The paper companies have forced entire towns to live in air that rotted out their lungs, as they did in Lincoln, Maine, by calling their stench "the smell of money.") The good people, aforesaid, think that the problems of an industrially underdeveloped region can be solved by raising its average income to the level of, say, Bayonne, New Jersey, or Gary, Indiana. It does no good to argue that a person can enjoy the blessings of that kind of life by moving there (and some of them do), and that many people are moving in the opposite direction because they do not prize the life that those good people would mark out for them. The argument seems to fail because it is not based solely on economic grounds. Puffins do not fit into profit-and-loss columns. And so it was necessary to set down a series of verbal equations to illustrate the cost-benefit ratio in bringing an oil development at this time to the Maine coast. This is the kind of work I got into first at Machiasport, and I set down a summary of some of our findings now because I believe that they have universal application.

II ❧ FOR ONE THING, Machias Bay was not a treasure about to yield itself up to the oilmen without some preliminary adjustments. The engineering firm hired by Bob Monks's Atlantic World Port to study the area concluded that one and perhaps two breakwaters would be needed to insure a safe haven for the mammoth tankers. The cost of a single breakwater would be eighty-six million dollars. "Some form of financial assistance—either from the state or federal government—would probably be necessary," the report said, "since contruction of the breakwaters by the operator of the facility would cause him to incur such a financial burden that the economic viability of the project might be jeopardized."

Some of the area's hazards were outlined by A. S. Mills, an experienced seaman, in a letter to the *Portland Press-Herald:*

> As a licensed pilot for any tonnage for that area, I can assure you that the problems are not simple. I frequently take vessels into the Navy dock at the Cutler Navy Radio Station, right across Machias Bay from the proposed dock site for the terminal at Machiasport, and it is not unusual to wait as much as two days for the undertow and surge to subside before being able to dock. The newly proposed dock site is in a much more exposed position and it is a sure bet that there would be extreme difficulty in holding a vessel of any size at a dock in this location. However, maybe the planners know something I don't know—I certainly hope so.

It is risky to pontificate on such matters, as the engineers who compiled the report for Atlantic World Port soon discovered. In December 1969 they announced, "We know of no major accidents that have affected the eastern seaboard." Less than two months later the tanker *Arrow* broke in half on the rocks of Chedabucto Bay, Nova Scotia, and poured 1.6 million gallons of oil into the sea and along the shoreline. But such accidents are infrequent, the oilmen used to say. Perhaps it was simply a coincidence, or perhaps it was greater attention to these things by the news media, but during the Machiasport controversy the sight of oily wastes oozing onto pristine beaches became as common on our television screens as that of chanting demonstrators and embattled GIs. The accidents continued to occur—in the most unlikely places, in clear weather and on calm seas—with depressing regularity. American tankers, according to an American Bureau of Shipping report, were involved in 570 collisions and groundings in the last decade; eighty-three per cent of these accidents took place inshore or while the ships were in port. And, according to the plans of the oilmen, at least two supertankers and ten smaller tankers were going to dock at Machiasport each week.

Accidents, many of them inexplicable, occur at even the smallest of the oil ports. I was reminded of an incident that struck close to home. It occurred at Jonesport in Washington County and I described it in an earlier book:*

Friday morning, December 4, 1964, was clear and cold on the Maine coast. A stiff wind blew, as it had most of the week, from the northeast. Oscar Carver, a lobster dealer on Beals Island, just across Mooseabec Reach from Jonesport on the mainland, left his office in a weathered frame building and walked down to the shore to look at his lobster pounds. What he saw first astonished and then nearly sickened him. Moving toward his pounds on the wind-and-tide-driven water was a broad, ugly, yellowish-black mass. His eyes quickly scanned the opposite shore. There, at anchor off Jonesport's oil storage depot, floated a large tanker. The oil, Oscar Carver realized, had escaped from the tanker during the discharging operation. Helplessly he watched the spreading mass blacken the offshore surf and then slowly begin to seep into his pounds. At that moment his lobster business was wiped out.

"It must have been five or six thousand gallons," Carver said later. "It got into my small pound first—the new one—and the lobsters just turned over and died. Then it got into the big pound. All week long after that the lobsters were crawling out of there up on the bank. I'd throw 'em back in the water, but they'd crawl right back out again and die on the bank."

* *Disaster by Default: Politics and Water Pollution*, M. Evans and Company, New York, 1966.

Oscar Carver and his wife were telling the story in the back room of their country store, which was now the only business they had left. "We piled up the lobsters on the bank for the gulls to eat," Mrs. Carver said, "but the gulls wouldn't eat them. Why, the oil was so thick on their shells you couldn't *wash* it off them."

"Most pitiful sight I ever saw," a neighbor said. "It was close to high tide when the oil floated up on the shore. Then when the tide turned the lobsters were trying to climb up on the shore to breathe and that oil just washed back over them, and the lobsters were dying right there."

Carver called the Coast Guard. "By the time we got the call the tanker had left," a Coast Guard officer said. "We sent investigators and they collected oil samples and took statements from available witnesses. This information was sent to the Corps of Engineers for further analysis and then to the Justice Department for final action."

Meanwhile, Carver was left with over 12,000 dead lobsters on his shore and an estimated loss of $20,000. The few surviving lobsters, their flesh badly tainted by oil, could not be sold for many months. He looked forward, eventually, to cleaning out his pounds, a long dirty job. (In court he received partial compensation for his loss.) But for at least a year Oscar Carver, who had been fishing for and dealing in lobsters for 25 years, would be out of the lobster business.

It is memories such as this that explain the hostility of Maine's fishermen to oil. The fear of a major spill in their fishing waters is compounded for them by the knowledge that the technology to contain or clean up such spills remains at the Stone Age level. For a while the oil industry counted on a variety of chemical dispersants to deal with a spill. These chemicals, which are designed to break up globs of oil, have been a bitter disappointment. Off Nova Scotia, for instance, where the icy water is of approximately the same temperature as that at Machiasport, the dispersants were not able to keep the oil from congealing into unsightly globs.

But the disillusionment with these chemicals went beyond their failure to do the job under certain harsh conditions. Scientists found that they were even more harmful to marine life than oil. This was proved after the *Torrey Canyon* disaster when chemical dispersants (mostly detergents) were used to fight the spill. Biological studies, widely publicized, disclosed that much of the damage to marine life was caused by the aromatic hydrocarbons in the detergents.

In Washington County, then, many men are gainfully and contentedly employed harvesting the sea's resources. For each job that a modern oil complex is likely to provide along the coast the inevitable spills are just as likely to wipe out several others. Fisheries sometimes are able to coexist with oil, but it's always an uneasy prospect.

"Anyone knows oil will float, and lobsters live on the bottom," one of oil's proponents said during the heat of battle. But this sort of old wives' tale was shattered by scientists a long time ago. Lobsters, like other species of shellfish, spend the early part of their lives floating on the surface with plankton. An oil spill is lethal to the young of all these species. Besides, oil adheres to dirt, sand, and detritus, and often sinks to the bottom, where toxic substances in the oil, hydrocarbons among them, can be ingested by bottom-dwelling species such as lobsters. And what sort of chain of events does that set off?

"We have studied the fate of organic compounds in the marine food chain," writes Dr. Max Blumer of Woods Hole Oceanographic Institution, "and have found that hydrocarbons, once they are incorporated into a particular marine organism, are stable, regardless of their structure, and that they may pass through many members of the marine food chain without alteration. . . . In the marine food chain hydrocarbons may not only be retained but they can actually be concentrated. This is a situation akin to that of the chlorinated pesticides."

Some of these substances, especially crude-oil residues such as high-boiling aromatic hydrocarbons, are similar to those found in tobacco tars and may be carcinogens (cancer-causing agents). Blumer believes that these substances could well be passed up the food chain to man.

Superficially, the battle was fought out between Bob Monks and the lobster fishermen. It is remarkable to organize lobstermen for any cause, and especially for the oil controversy, which was essentially a political struggle. Lobstermen are, for instance, notoriously delinquent in their voting habits. Election Day falls during the peak period of the fall lobster season, just when the traps are filling up and the fishermen are eager to haul as often as possible before winter's onset. Many lobstermen even detest the idea of registering to vote, because they would become liable for jury duty and perhaps lose a couple of weeks during the season. Despite this tendency, and their reputation as taciturn and independent-spirited Yankees, the lobster fishermen not only organized to some extent to fight oil, but several of them proved to be eloquent and resourceful campaigners.

Jasper Cates, a lobsterman and sometime versifier from Cutler, set the tone during a public meeting in Machias:

> We strongly oppose refineries being placed anywhere in this area because they carry an unacceptable amount of risk to our livelihoods, our environment, and our way of life. Placing them in this area we feel would be incompatible not only with conditions that exist in the world today, but with the way we wish to develop this area. The oil industry constitutes a cruel hoax against the hopes and needs of the mostly unskilled poor and hungry people in our midst. They want industries suitable to the area and to their abilities. They want something that will help them, not ruin them. It has been said that a hungry man will grasp for straws, but I say that unless he is crazy he won't reach for a tiger.

Barna Norton, who is Jonesport's harbor master, made himself effective in a number of ways. After he had visited the scene of the big spill at Chedabucto Bay in Nova Scotia, he reported back to his colleagues about the mess along the coast: "The weird thing was that there were no birds along the shore," he said. "I saw a sardine cannery—and there wasn't a gull even sitting on the roof!"

Norton went to the trouble to take pictures at various times of Stone Island, where the Machiasport terminal was to be located, and the more protected islands nearby. The photographs were revealing: on the shore of the protected islands driftwood and other debris gathered while plants sprouted from their rocky faces; but Stone Island, completely open to winds from the easterly quarter, was swept clean of both debris and plants.

Monks, clinging to the theory that what's in the average person's mind is what's put there, embarked on an energetic promotion campaign to sell an oil complex to Washington County. He made friendly overtures to the lobstermen. He invited a small party of Washington County people (including lobstermen and newspapermen) to visit a spanking-new "clean" oil refinery in the Virgin Islands to see its innocuousness at first hand; this plan fizzled when a spy-conscious armed guard turned back the visitors at the refinery's gates, compelling them to repair to a nearby hillside, where all they could do was gaze down on all that gleaming hardware and sniff the ambient air, which proved to be wholesome that day. Monks also conducted a plebiscite in Machiasport and a few surrounding towns to determine the local citizens' feelings about oil. To prepare the public for the vote he bought time on a Machias radio station one Saturday afternoon and went on the air to answer listeners' telephone questions about the proposed oil complex.

The radio program infuriated a number of lobstermen, who felt that Monks and his associates had distorted the picture. The fishermen raised money to buy time for a program of their own, which was aired on a succeeding Saturday and consisted of a panel which I was invited to join. We had four lobstermen, a couple of state biologists, a representative of the

Governor's office (the only panelist who was pro-oil), myself, and Harbor Master Barna Norton of Jonesport, who served as moderator. We assembled around a table in the broadcast room. A microphone hung from the ceiling on a long cord, and when a question was asked by a caller from outside, the man who wanted to answer it reached for the microphone and spoke his piece. Inevitably, when one of us had finished speaking, the Governor's representative reached for the microphone to make a rebuttal. After this had gone on for a short time, moderator Norton took matters (or rather, the microphone) into his own hands. When one of us had made a point, Norton would simply draw the microphone firmly to himself and proceed to the next question while the Governor's man gestured and grimaced in frustration. Dissent was effectively stifled, and the anti-oil forces enjoyed an uninterruptedly loquacious afternoon. Monks, however, held on to his early lead in the unofficial plebiscite to win approval for his plans at Machiasport by a handful of the twenty-five hundred votes cast.

III 🌿 ANOTHER FORCE had entered the public debate, a force whose importance, I think, might be underestimated. This was a new state-wide weekly newspaper called the *Maine Times*. Its editor, John N. Cole, was a refugee from Long Island, New York, who had been the editor of a local paper around Brunswick before attempting to fill a communications vacuum throughout Maine. Before Cole, some lights of intelligence were discernible here and there throughout the state, as in Portland, or where a competent editor had established a local weekly, but on the whole the state's press stood in monolithic blandness. Such were the shock waves put in motion by the appearance of intelligence, hard questions and investigative reporting that for a time the *Maine Times*, for all its good taste and restraint, often was described contemptuously by local exploiters as "an underground newspaper."

Cole looked at all aspects of the state within the framework of its environment—hardly an original viewpoint, but revolutionary under the conditions that ruled Maine when the newspaper began publication late in 1968. It was Cole's purpose "to keep Maine from becoming an extension of the no-place that so much of the eastern United States has become . . . to help make Maine the place that makes living here such a special kind of life." The *Times* layout and typography are attractive, its prose is usually graceful (despite the sentence just quoted). Its circulation grew rapidly, and by the end of 1971 it reached fifteen thousand, a figure that circulation experts say insures a paper readership of over fifty thousand people once each issue has been passed around among family and friends. That is a significant figure in a state of one million people.

But beyond that is the paper's influence. It is read by many of the state's policy-makers and trend-setters, including the editors and staff members of other publications. Thus the *Maine Times* has set a new standard for even the most backward of its competitors. Stories once left untouched because of laziness or timidity are suddenly appearing on the front pages of other newspapers. It seems to me that the *Bangor Daily News* (which serves the entire northern half of the state) increased in both diligence and sophistication within a year or so of the *Times'* introduction, and I am always pleased to see the *News* pick up an important story that appeared first in Cole's weekly paper.

That the *Maine Times* had made its mark was quickly confirmed when Bob Monks, hankering for high political office, began to pay court to Cole. Cole was along on Monks's Cessna for the trip to a public meeting at Machias. After Monks leaped into politics, challenging Margaret Chase Smith for her seat in the Senate, Cole's nonprofit Allagash

Group was the recipient of those options that Monks held on Machiasport's strategic land, an Allagash Group committee having been appointed to find ways in which the options could best be used for Washington County's benefit; and though Cole was openly anti-oil, his paper contributed to Monks's self-portrait as a glamorous, civic-minded young man. The *Maine Times* attested to Monks's concern for Maine's people and environment, and applauded Monks's insistence on a comprehensive land-use plan to save the Maine coast. Cole, whose standard of excellence was forcing the rest of Maine's press to toe the mark, also was sketching Monks's portrait in heroic dimensions, a standard that the young millionaire may be obliged to live up to, to Maine's enduring well-being.

—

And so, in a hundred ways Maine people were being made aware of the variety of issues that were involved at Machiasport. Even those local citizens who were most outspoken in favor of the oil complex always qualified their support by including the insistence that the state must stipulate "proper pollution controls" before giving its blessing to such a scheme. (It is instructive to note that economy-minded voters in Maine turned down referenda to provide additional financing for two erstwhile inviolate issues—higher education and highway building—during this period, and yet approved two major bond issues for water-pollution control.) This broadening of the public's awareness was not merely an acknowledgment that pollution existed, as it was in so many other parts of the country, but also a premonition of paradise lost. Until oil and Machiasport focused national attention on Washington County, many of its residents took the coast and its treasures for granted. Suddenly the television cameramen were on the scene, shooting "mood" footage and expressing the wonder that men and women from other parts of the country felt on looking at this very special part of the world. For the first time many Down Easters ceased to look upon themselves as forgotten denizens of the nation's backwater. They experienced a new sense of their own worth. Just as the people of an earlier century saw the wilderness composed into a coherent and picturesque reality for them by their landscape painters, so people in Washington County first responded consciously to their own land when it was shown to them in living color on their television sets.

Perhaps the most spectacular awakening of all took place in September 1970, when Senator Muskie brought his Subcommittee on Air and Water Pollution to Machias "to provide a forum for the discussion of these critical issues in the communities that may be affected." The two-day hearing was held in Powers Hall at Washington State College (now the University of Maine at Machias). All of the issues and arguments were trotted out for the committee's inspection. Local businessmen cited the county's economic troubles as an argument for oil, the lobstermen cited oil's potential hazards as an argument against it. The industry's public-relations men bustled about the auditorium in their sharkskin suits, courting the press and cutting each other's throats. Scientists read their papers on fish kills and laboratory tests.

The conflict was perhaps most effectively dramatized by the opposite sides taken by labor officials (a rare species in any case in Washington County): a man from the Maine Federated Labor Council correlated the county's woes with its low level of industrial development, while a man from the Oil, Chemical and Atomic Workers International Union warned the people of Machiasport about the "silent violence" that refinery operators perpetrate against workers and nearby residents in the form of poisonous effluents.

"Do I gather that, if what is involved is a typical refinery, you would not recommend it for Machiasport?" Muskie asked Anthony Mazzocchi, the Citizenship-Legislative Director of the Oil Workers Union.

"I think the industry has to do better than they have done before we can assume that the integrity of the environment will be protected," Mazzocchi replied. "I must say this, in all fairness: that people have to make a decision. If they are for economic enhancement, there is no doubt that a refinery would accomplish this. I do not think, though, that you can protect and preserve the environment in its present state with the addition of an oil refinery. I think the two are rather inconsistent."

"In other words," Muskie prodded, "a refinery, in your experience, is not clean, environmentally."

"No, it is absolutely not," Mazzocchi said. "Experience with refineries in America, contrary to the big ads that the industry pays for, demonstrates just the opposite."

At the end of the hearings, Muskie earned the respect of many of his critics by reversing publicly his earlier stand. Having examined the available evidence, he told the press that he could no longer support an oil complex in eastern Maine at the present stage of our technology.

17

MAKING IT

ONE MAN HAD changed his mind, but many more had not. Those who struggle to save a natural resource or a way of life are nearly always at a disadvantage. They argue on aesthetic grounds, which seem frivolous to their opponents, or on matters of public health, which are seldom effective unless bodies, deceased or deformed, can be introduced as evidence. A person may even be sympathetic to these arguments, may donate money to save wildlife in Africa or a forest half a continent away, may vote for clean air and water in his state; but when he detects an economic issue close to home, he is willing to put up with "a little pollution." The most effective opponents of an oil complex in Washington County were not conservationists or scientists or summer people. They were the lobster fishermen, who were fighting on economic grounds.

It was important, then, that in compiling our arguments we countered the economic claims of Monks and the other oilmen. We wanted to learn, in view of the threat to the shore, whether the economic benefits promised to the county were substantial. Many of the local residents were already worried about the impact of a sudden influx of oil workers and their families on the local school systems, police departments, and other public services. Machiasport, or whatever town was chosen as the site of the industrial complex, would have its tax base expanded many times over. But it was not likely that the people who came to work at the complex would want to live in its immediate neighborhood. Thus the burden of providing services for these people would fall on other towns not financially able to deal with them. It has been the case in other boom towns, over and over again, that the taxes paid by a flood of new residents do not compensate for the demands these people make on public services.

What of the savings to local people in gasoline and fuel oil if a refinery settled in their midst? It has not been the case that the price of gasoline or other oil products is appreciably lower close to the country's major oil centers than it is in New England. Nor were the oilmen themselves (Monks among them) optimistic about savings. It did not take us long to realize that the uncertainties of the oil-import system, the faded chances of bringing a foreign-trade zone to Machiasport in view of the Western oilmen's opposition, the soaring insurance rates on giant tankers, and the built-in costs of proper pollution control suddenly demanded by the state, all considerably eroded the savings that the project's spokesmen had originally promised the local consumer.

But would this manifestation of progress bring other benefits to a county that had been branded as "underdeveloped"? Speaking of another state, Murray Kempton once said, "It is not how far it has advanced, but how many people it has left behind." There are poverty and decay in the county, but I have never seen an oil refinery abolish blight in any area of the country; slums flourish in the vicinity of refineries, as they do around most other heavy industries. A modern oil refinery, by the industry's own testimony, provides comparatively few jobs, and the most important ones are filled by experienced hands from the country's great oil-producing centers. Admittedly, there will still be jobs for local residents. But poverty exists in Washington County chiefly among those who, because of age, infirmity, disposition, or lack of skills and aptitudes, will not be able to take advantage of the job opportunities in a modern refinery. The Canadians, who have had considerable experience in government-encouraged industrialization that was designed to give a lift to poor areas, supply some guidance here. A report issued by the New Brunswick Task Force on Social Development at the end of 1971 said:

> Because the federal government is further removed from the citizen than the provincial government, many feel that some programs are imposed without consultation and often with an almost total unawareness of local needs. Manpower programs, for example, do not necessarily help the person who has little education and few skills. Some believe them to be primarily economic in their orientation rather than social, and as a consequence, those who have real needs in terms of training are denied it.

Clearly, alternative solutions must be found to provide for these people. They are the ones for whom statistics dealing with low income levels are meaningful, not the able-bodied of the county. Unemployment statistics distort the picture. These statistics are relevant in industrialized areas, such as Bangor, where the collapse of the shoe industry has thrown out of work many men and women dependent on a steady income. It is more difficult to find genuinely unemployed people in Washington County, because the figures include men and women who work only seasonally and who would not work full-time under any circumstances.

"Who the hell wants to work full time?" a local man was quoted in a county newspaper. "I would rather work for myself part time than be owned by some company for two weeks' vacation each year. Life is too damn short." And another: "At present in our town there is not one unemployed person. I have more work than I can handle. I'll be glad when bad weather comes so I can get a breather."

In fact, there is a shortage of skilled workers of nearly every kind. For a while it was thought that only "summer people" couldn't find a carpenter or an electrician. Now people who have lived here all their lives ask *me* if I can locate a skilled worker of some kind for them. Garages in the area complain that they cannot locate competent mechanics to handle the demand for repairs. Several years ago a young carpenter from Massachusetts married a woman here and settled down in the community to live and work. Now he has more work than he can accept and there is a waiting list for his services, a situation that is repeated almost endlessly throughout the county.

To clamp on a huge modern industry, upsetting the delicate balances within both the society and its environment, is as silly as mounting a jet aircraft engine on a motorbike. "What have we got here, about twenty-eight thousand people?" a man who works for the State Extension Service asked one day while we were talking about the county's problems. "Take out the children and the housewives and the retired people, and what's left? You could stick two or three small plants around the county that would employ about forty people each and you'd take care of most of the people who still want steady employment."

Moreover, the differences in annual average incomes between Washington County and other regions cited by the oil spokesmen are often illusory. There are some frightful instances of poverty here—people living in shacks with dirt floors and inadequate heating—but these instances are found among the people who simply cannot fend for themselves under any conditions. This is a national problem that can be dealt with only by professional men and women who bring both skills and compassion to the task. Among the able-bodied poor in this county there is not the same level of poverty that one finds in the cities. These people know how to extract food and fuel from the land. Most of them own their own homes, grow part of their own food, hunt and fish for more of it, and cut their own firewood.

Even the basis for compiling accurate income statistics in this area, as in any resource-rich economy, is deficient. Many residents, being unsalaried, keep only the sketchiest records for the tax collector. No one knows how much they earn supplying goods and services to their neighbors and the summer people. A vivid illustration of this was recounted to me several years ago by a lawyer who had undertaken a case for some fishermen in another state.

"Pollution was ruining their fishing grounds," the lawyer told me, "and we could pinpoint the source of the pollution exactly. It was an open-and-shut case, and I took it to court to get the pollution stopped. But the polluters had a smart lawyer. He said that if the fishermen claimed that his client was wrecking their business, then they had to show economic loss. He demanded to see their books. The fishermen weren't keeping records and they weren't paying taxes, so they told me to back off. I had to drop the case."

In our area the residents usually pay their taxes, but there are so many supplements to their cash incomes (including barter in one form or another, as, for instance, the trading of services for goods) that the Department of Economic Development's figures on poverty levels are misleading. Theories and programs applicable to Harlem or Seattle or Appalachia will not work in Washington County. Politics, sociology, philanthropy, and ecology abound in recent case histories that illustrate the folly of imposing hasty and inappropriate solutions on a people or a place.

This is not to suggest that the advice of the conservationists, the scientists, or the summer people is wholly welcome around here, either. Outsiders, even those who are boosters or progress-at-any-price developers in their own communities, will come to a place like eastern Maine and try to hold the clock back. They want to see only graceful old houses, unspoiled vistas, and local people acting out their lives with quaint mannerisms. For their part, local boosters look on conservationists as the contemporary carpetbaggers. They resent pleas for preservation as an attempt to consign their region to "environmental oblivion." This is nothing new, of course. G. M. Trevelyan,* referring to nineteenth-century England, wrote that "enclosure of the commons was ultimately stopped not by the protest of the rural peasantry, but of the urban population, who objected to exclusion from its holiday playgrounds and rural breathing spaces." The people who are moving to rural areas today exert their own pressures to bring about an environment that is congenial to themselves. Anthony Bailey† has written of this conflict between two sets of interests in his own town in Connecticut, where "the Yankees are always planting trees wherever they can, and it is the Portuguese of the borough street-cleaning crew who have to sweep up the leaves."

———

Though I have, as it were, one foot in Washington County and the other outside, I can sympathize with the difficulties of making a living here. Most writers, if they are not on the staff of a publication, retain a connection with a university or live within commuting distance of their publishing contacts in a large city. I had my contacts in New York when I came to Maine, but I was not an "established" writer who had prepared himself for such a move with large cash reserves and a series of writing projects already contracted for. A novelist or a painter, who carries his material locked in his own vision and imagination, is better equipped to stretch the umbilical cord that links him with the sources of his income. But a free-lance writer of nonfiction books and articles needs to keep in touch more closely with the outside world to collect his assignments and carry on his research.

* *English Social History*, Longmans, Green and Company, New York, 1943.
† *In the Village*, Alfred A. Knopf, New York, 1971.

Thus the step into eastern Maine demanded a certain risk. Could I make a living here? On the available evidence, the answer had to be no; there was the county's reputation as a place that was hard even for a native to make a living in, and there were the comments I had already heard from summer residents and visitors, on the order of "I'd love to settle down here, but of course there'd be no way for me to pay the grocery bill."

But security has never been among my obsessions. When I was working for the New York *Sun* as a copy boy during summer vacations from Columbia my colleagues and I were willing to put up with ridiculously low wages and all sorts of curious chores in the hope that some day we would go to work as reporters for that noble (but alas, moribund) institution. For the twenty-three dollars a week the *Sun* paid us, we had to approach every job in the way they had done it for nearly a century there, which included taking our turn once a week to push a cart through the streets and collect the paper's daily mail at the post office; several copy boys thought this beneath the dignity of young college men, especially if they happened to be seen by one of their girl friends or fraternity brothers, and one of us even suggested that we "strike for higher pay, shorter hours, and the right to pee in the streets like the horses." But these indignities did not diminish our enthusiasm for the *Sun*. In fact, it made a lasting impression on me to learn, one day, that a bright young copy boy was quitting to take a similarly menial job at *Time*. It seemed that he didn't want to leave the *Sun*, but the old paper had no pension plan, and *Time* did. I was horrified. Only twenty-one years old, and my friend was fitting his life into the strait jacket of an old-age pension plan!

So, as Ada and I talked it over during that first autumn in Maine, we admitted there was a risk, but it was not overwhelming. I certainly did not want a "career." (A life can grow, a career can only be *furthered*.) And five hundred miles linked for most of their length by modern highways and an airline would not isolate me like a man in Tibet. At first, living in the camp, we were nearly five miles from the nearest telephone. One optimistic editor thought he could keep in touch with me by telegram, but since I had no phone the Western Union office at Bar Harbor merely stuffed the urgent messages into envelopes and mailed them to me.

As a sop to fortune, we invested for a couple of years in a small New York apartment out of which I was able to operate when on an extended assignment and which we subleased during the rest of the year. What would I write about? Perhaps Alexander Woollcott's summing up of the writer's agony is most exquisite: "I was the best writer in America. It's just that I had nothing to say." The American public was not even aware that it had an environment at the time, so the market for conservation articles was limited. But I had always enjoyed writing about sports, especially nostalgic pieces (just as the older a man gets the faster he ran as a boy, so the mightier his early heroes loom up out of the past), and I enjoyed writing for young readers. Sometimes I combined these two interests, writing books about baseball for children.

In recent years I have been able to devote most of my time to my special interests in the natural world. From our experiences in directing a children's nature center for the town on a voluntary basis, Ada and I derived the ideas for a number of books about that natural world for young readers.

Ada, before joining me in the literary life, had taught grammar school for a couple of years in a town in nearby Hancock County. This was not wholly successful because the local powers apparently were squeamish about educating their future masters. Ada found more freedom and satisfaction later on in a summer Head-Start program organized in Washington County in the face of the authorities' less-than-enthusiastic response. There is a genuine fear here of the "permissiveness" that has produced a generation of hoodlums and bomb-throwers in the cities (drugs are available, though not yet a serious problem). But distinctions are being made so that the school system no longer fully equates rote and discipline with education, even for five-year-olds. It is possible to be a teacher in Washington County.

It is true that there are still visitors to the county who detect only starkness in the landscape and decay in the society. Outsiders often see the local people as stereotypes, as taciturn, emotionless Yankees, crafty and suspicious. They fail to distinguish liveliness from emotion. I dispute the widely held assumption that Falstaff is more "human" than, let's say, Malvolio, that a hearty appetite, a prodigious thirst, high color and full lips, a garrulous disposition, and conspicuous promiscuity render a character (in either fiction or "real life") more human, and therefore more interesting, than his pallid contemporaries. A wastrel need not be any more human than a prudent bank president (though he may be more of an animal).

It has been my experience that most of the people in our area, natives and newcomers alike, feel we have come as close as possible, within the limitations of our own resources, to attaining a good life. I have seen a sense of satisfaction that is not shiftlessness but security. One has reached the home port, and found it not a cul-de-sac but a bay of endless variety. Not everyone is capable of joy, but there is as much of it here as in most other places, and often it is the joy that is rooted in the deepest experiences, in a family life that has not yet been shaken apart by a dislocated society, and in a relationship with the natural world that is not filtered through a television screen.

Our region's anachronisms leave it vulnerable. No one who has driven across the Pulaski Skyway in New Jersey can help remaining skeptical about the assurances that an oil refinery can improve the quality of our lives. There survives in our midst, it is true, the very human hope that our lives can be enriched by having a new order imposed on us from above. There is also impatience that the better life does not evolve faster from within.

The pressures are increasing. Recently the oilmen's focus has shifted to Eastport, where a powerful conglomerate, the Pittston Company, plans to build a terminal and refinery. The saddest remark I heard during the long controversy over oil in Washington County was made by Dana Jacobs, a decent man who is the city manager of Eastport: "Eastport needs the oil industry," he told a state legislative committee, "to help us finance our pollution-abatement facilities."

PART ✻ SIX
A Margin to Life

18
DOOMSDAY RECONSIDERED

DOOMSDAY IS UPON US, the computers insist. The effects of unrestricted growth now transcend local areas to merge in a global menace. Pollution and population push us to the breaking point, as remorseless as Regan and Goneril. The news has led to a certain amount of hand-wringing, but in general men and women have taken such tidings in stride, as they once went on matter-of-factly in licentiousness while their priests thundered fire and brimstone at them, trusting to set it all right at the last hour. Ecological collapse and nuclear holocaust might, like perdition, prove to be finally but a nightmare vision of the fanatics.

Where does the truth lie? It is always well to accord the doom-sayers a measure of respect, if only to placate the evil spirits, but it seems to me that those who predict some sort of imminent catastrophe for civilization, some global "killer smog," some great cleansing disaster, are really the optimists. For then the survivors, whether they are people or simply warm little blobs on a mudbank, could dig themselves out of the rubble and begin building a brighter, cleaner world.

I am a pessimist. I see a different sort of catastrophe ahead. I see blight creeping like a stain. The ultimate horror is not total collapse, but man's successful adaptation to the joyless homogeneity that characterizes so great a part of our Atlantic and Pacific coasts today. (Not many years ago, one-third of this country's population lived within fifty miles of the coast; by the year 2000, that figure will rise to two-thirds.) If the wrong decisions are made in the future, as they were in the past, there will be little left of our physical and spiritual heritage. Progress at any cost will subtract at a faster and faster rate from the marvelous diversity of our world, a diminution that will, I believe, turn us into something less than human.

But one cannot go on acting on hopeless assumptions. As more Americans achieve some degree of affluence, they will begin to make different decisions about the kind of life they want for themselves and their children. In the past their decisions, ill-conceived or taken out of ignorance, contributed to our present decay. But ideas and information are open to more people today than ever before, as they were to the Reverend Charles Dorchester and his friends when they decided to fight oil at Machiasport. The steps toward a richer life will vary in detail from one area of the country to another, but I think that in their broad outlines they will reflect the experience that many people have had in Maine. If the blight is to be contained, action will take place on both the national and local level.

In the absence of any national policy by the federal government about where we are going and how we are going to get there (a policy that should be based on the best current knowledge of the experts and approved by the people themselves) every part of the country is prey to haphazard development. When a social or economic crisis is discerned, the myopic authorities tack on to the area the largest and most expensive gimcrack they can wheedle out of the people who hold the pursestrings. Their remedy in most cases is simply a short-term solution to the region's problems, which is probably destructive in the long run. Alvin Toffler, in *Future Shock*,* suggests that these technocrats must learn to extend their "time horizons":

> If a region needs electricity, they reach for a power plant. The fact that such a plant might sharply alter labor patterns, that within a decade might throw men out of work, force large-scale retraining of workers, and swell the social welfare costs of a nearby city—such considerations are too remote in time to concern them. The fact that the plant could trigger devastating ecological consequences a generation later simply does not register in their time frame.

Early in this century the men who made the decisions nationally and locally destroyed a lovely valley, Hetch Hetchy, in Yosemite National Park in order to solve San Francisco's water problems. John Muir had called this remote mountain valley "a wonderfully exact counterpart of the great Yosemite, not only in its crystal river and sublime rocks and waterfalls, but in the gardens, groves, and meadows of its flowery, park-like floor." Unfortunately, San Francisco's engineers thought that the valley's steep cliffs and its "flowery, park-like floor" would form a perfectly marvelous container, or reservoir, in which the water of its "crystal river" could be stored for the city's use. Despite the bitter opposition of conservationists, the engineers built their dam at Hetch Hetchy. That they could have solved the problem by taking water from alternate sources in the mountains carried little weight with these men when they calculated that by destroying Hetch Hetchy they would save a few dollars. Today, when Hetch Hetchy would have been a priceless addition to Yosemite's overburdened attractions, we realize that the "experts" made a terrible mistake. Nor did they (or their

* Random House, New York, 1970.

intellectual descendants) learn from that mistake. They were just as eager to sacrifice Everglades National Park in the 1960s in a short-term solution to Miami's transportation problem. But some of the people had learned. The outcry against a mammoth jetport that would have severed or contaminated the Everglades' water supply caused the bureaucrats to revise their idiotic plan.

In this age of efficiency, it strikes the bureaucrats as heresy when "the people" challenge the decisions that they feel they have been trained to make. What is the fatal flaw that turns the bureaucrats' best-laid plans awry? Probably it has never been expressed any better than by an anonymous contributor to England's *The Economist* more than a century ago.*

> There is a certain Pharisaism of intellect which is created or fostered by the habits of official, and especially of departmental life. It is a dangerous thing for a man to live with all the official data he can want for any decisions always within his reach, docketed in pigeon-holes, with intellectual laborers always at his command to search, investigate and condense for him. . . . They hold themselves culpably deficient in self respect if they listen at all to the lessons of popular conviction.

But popular conviction will need certain facts and guidelines if it is to lead us out of our present mess. It is in this area, with the public's consent, that the federal government can play its proper role. For instance, many people know that if we are to keep our world from drowning in an excess of pollution, we will have to pay more for the goods whose production contributes to that pollution. By forcing the producers to install the latest antipollution devices, government will insure that they include *all* of the production costs (part of which have until now been the environmental degradation charged off to the public at large) when they set the wholesale price for their goods. Conversely, consumers will be encouraged to buy,

* *The Economist,* 5 February 1859.

and producers to make, goods that are not polluters per se. Then we may see a shift back to the products made from natural raw materials rather than the synthetics that are causing much of the trouble.

As we try to cure our local problems (not only in Maine but elsewhere around the country), we are learning that there is an urgent need for a national energy policy. The country's present fragmentary policies encourage us to deplete our natural resources, as well as to build a variety of installations (dams, power plants, oil refineries) as short-term solutions— but long-term disasters.

The lack of any such national policy contributed to the confusion at Machiasport. The major result of the public concern there was not in its effect on the final decision of whether to build or not to build. It was, rather, a warning to the authorities that they must take these projects' social and environmental impact into consideration in the future. And, in truth, the ultimate decision at Machiasport was made not on the spot but in Washington, when President Richard M. Nixon decided to delay any action on the controversial oil-import quotas. Without its foreign oil to refine, Occidental had no need for a refinery there. The specter of oil at Machiasport faded into oblivion, at least temporarily, in the early 1970s. But the uproar started by the conservationists at Machiasport has delayed, and in some cases permanently blocked, oil installations at other inappropriate places along the coast.

If the nation ever devises a sound national energy policy it must include two vital steps: the experts will be encouraged to measure our energy demands for the future and, even more important, to try to temper those demands. Today the experts predict that our energy consumption during the last thirty years of this century will be three times the total consumed during the preceding thirty years. In 1970, when there was practically no growth in our gross national product, the country's energy consumption rose a dramatic 4.5 per cent over the previous year to 69,000 trillion Btu (British thermal units); it is estimated that in the year 2000 this total will reach 170,000 trillion Btu.

Someone has defined planning as "the organization of shortage." It will fall to the federal government to organize the inevitable shortages, not only of fossil fuels but of suitable sites for locating major installations such as refineries and power plants. The critical decisions in our society are still based on economics. Fighting fire with fire, then, the government must eventually combat both shortage and pollution by regulating the consumption of energy in economic terms. This course will mean devising schemes to raise the price we pay for power.

Such schemes will be directed not simply at the homeowner who uses power to run appliances (and even frills such as electric toothbrushes and electric carving knives) but, more to the point, at the major industrial consumers. At present many industries are able to buy power cheaply because they use it in great quantities. Economies of scale of this sort will probably have to be abolished by federal laws in order to restrict runaway consumption. Similarly, the federal government will have to cooperate with the various states in spacing out the new power plants that the experts predict will be built to supply our demands by the end of the century. Under present projections, these power plants will rise along the Hudson River and some other waterways like utility poles along a roadway, warming and contaminating the water to an intolerable degree.

"We will have to learn to avoid the vulnerable aspects of the environment," a scientist says. "We should be taking advantage of its flexible aspects."

These national decisions, when we keep in mind the complexity of human beings and the natural world around them, will make it possible for us to deal effectively with what we think of as local problems today. We won't rush frenziedly to sink oil wells off our coasts as a short-term solution to our economic problems. We will recognize not only the environmental hazards of such a course, but also the great initial financial costs and the lengthy time lag between the beginning of the search for oil and its eventual production. Enormous reserves must be present to make offshore extraction feasible. Two to five years are needed for such exploration. Off the northeastern coast bad weather will restrict drilling for a good part of the year. Six to nine years may elapse from the time oilmen discover a reserve under the ocean until they are able to get a small rig into operation.

To drill or not to drill, to build or not to build, to consume or not to consume—these are some of the questions that a national energy policy will consider. National decisions (in which all the people of the country take a part) will affect local issues in the other problems we have been talking about, too. Only the federal government can regulate destructive cutting practices in our national forests and thus set a standard for the foresters on private land. Only the federal government can establish a national farm policy that will mitigate some of the present evils of the system; among these evils are the forces that drive out the small farmer, keeping millions of acres of land out of production at great cost to the taxpayers while encouraging such intensive farming on the remainder that the growers must resort to the excessive and deleterious use of pesticides, fertilizers, and even water itself.

Ultimately, many of the national problems will become manageable if they are seen in the context of a sensible program of land use. On the federal level this means that the government will retain remnants of the public domain, classifying them so that they will be used in such a way that *all* Americans will benefit from them. It will also move to protect forever the country's estuarine areas and other shorelines, including those of the Great Lakes, from the bulldozers and the land-fillers. The states themselves have, in general, failed to force the needed shoreline zoning by local communities. I think that only a centralized federal authority can bring to this the overview that will take into consideration the complexities of our coastline. The exploiters, of course, will fight these land-use decisions to the death, raging about wilderness lovers and bird watchers. (Whenever a man uses "bird watcher" as an epithet, you can be sure that he is defending himself against those who would stop him from squeezing an illicit dollar from the land.)

Locally, the question of what use to make of our land will be even more difficult to answer. The pressures are strong to make hasty and irrevocable decisions. The quality of our lives will depend on what those decisions are.

19

CORNERS
AND CRANNIES

THIS WOULD HAVE BEEN a different, and probably a more reassuring, book had I written it ten years ago. I would have crowded it with portraits of flinty-eyed, quaint-talking lobstermen, with passages about the fog slipping in from the sea to envelop some headland's bare and menacing shoulders, with definitions of local words (thrumcap,* pokelogan†) coined and preserved in isolation. When the narrative flagged I would have inserted cherished examples of Down East wit and wisdom culled from one of the fat little notebooks that writers compile for such purposes. I would have banished outsiders from my book's pages, except when I wanted a foil against which to show off one of my prize local specimens.

But modern America, vibrating with a force that sometimes might even be life, has overflowed into this land. Here we

* A small, tree-tufted island said to resemble the caps once made from thrum (the fringe of warp left over on a loom).
† A loggers' term, apparently a corruption of the words "pouch" and "lagoon," for any small bay along a river's shore.

227

move to the same beat that throbs in the consciousness of our fellows in Colorado, or Iowa, or Arkansas, or New Jersey. This, too, is life in America during the final third of the twentieth century, no matter how distractedly some of us push these inklings away. Whether we live in the ghetto, entombed in filth, blare and crime, or in some leafy exurban countryside, we share a preoccupation with the quality of our lives. Can we seize the choices that are open to us? Are we equipped to make the right decisions?

Here in Maine, we fend off the oilmen, crying that our pristine coast should be preserved so that it can fulfill the purpose for which God created it—as a fair-weather haven for the cramped millions just to the south and west of us. The implication is that tourists are clean, and that oilmen are not. If Machiasport is not to become Bayonne, New Jersey, can it remain Shangri-la?

Not long ago an organization of businessmen asked me to come and talk to them about the environment during their annual gathering, which was to be held in Acapulco, Mexico. As I was preparing to leave with Ada for a week with the businessmen, by chance I came upon the following passage in an essay written over half a century ago by H. M. Tomlinson, that Englishman who captured the romance of merchant ships, their ports, and the sea perhaps better than anyone else who has ever written about them:

You probably know there are place-names which, when whispered privately, have the unreasonable power of translating the spirit east of the sun and west of the moon. They cannot be seen in print without a thrill. The names in the atlas which do that for me are a motley lot, and you, who see no magic in them, but have your own lunacy in another phase, would laugh at mine. Celebes, Acapulco, Para, Port Royal, Cartagena, the Marquesas, Panama, the Mackenzie River, Tripoli or Barbary. They are some of mine. Rome should be there, I know, and Athens, and Byzantium. But they are not, and that is all I can say about it.

Yes, there it is, right up near the top of the list, I thought. For Tomlinson himself, only fifty years ago, it was a golden name, perhaps making his heart beat a little faster when his finger, tracing exotic coastlines, came upon it one night as he sat with a map open on his knees in his study in a London suburb. Almost within my lifetime men could dream dreams about magic landfalls under an ardent sun, and Acapulco would be among them. And their dreams would have a basis in fact, for sailors must have brought home tales of that marvelous bay cupped in the Sierra Madre del Sur where they plunged into the sea. Now I would be able to see for myself.

The reality of Acapulco proved to be depressing. It was like entering one of those nightclubs, the façade promising glamorous exoticism and dimly lit sin, to find that somebody has turned on all the lights and only the shabby pasteboard and tinny spangles remain. Most of the high-priced hotels were set along a narrow, unappetizing beach, solidly anchored not in romance but in a contemporary "miracle mile." The ambience, far from the stuff of dreams, was instead the roar and stench of motor traffic, the décor was dominated by sleazy hamburger joints; even the legendary bay was polluted. Had I blundered into Cleveland? Dayton? Perhaps even Bangor?

Few of the major hotels' clientele ever even asked themselves such questions I would think, because they never seemed to leave poolside or the hotel cocktail lounges. What was it that stayed with them from their Acapulco vacation to make it different from an evening on the town back in Memphis or Omaha? How many of them could have encountered any experience they would not have found in either place at the appropriate time of year? I am not denying that there were tourists besides myself who had come looking for a new experience, to touch a different way of life. But the tourist industry that lured us there had paved over and blotted out the essence that had created a golden aura around Acapulco in the first place.

Only with a second look, only by detaching ourselves from

the spangled pasteboard, were Ada and I able to take home with us the certainty that this was not Dayton or Bangor. As we walked to the terminal from the plane that first day, I saw long-tailed, glossy-black birds feeding on the lawn. Grackles, I shrugged, and what else is new? Then I took a second look and detected the swollen, ridged bill that surely never graced a grackle. I had seen my first groove-billed ani, a tropical cuckoo the northern limits of whose range barely touch our southwestern border.

And so in every free moment we sought out the remnants of the natural world that had so far endured (or adapted to) man's otherwise successful attempt to smooth over regional differences. We watched, as it soared over the beach near our hotel, a frigate bird (probably the "sky-hawk" that, nailed to the mainmast and wrapped in Ahab's flag, was the living part of heaven that went down in the vortex with the *Pequod*). We visited the golf course to look at the tropical trees and shrubs, and the hummingbirds, caciques, and orioles that set their foliage afire. And we found a couple of boys who took us by boat into the lagoon and the mangrove jungles to watch the creatures of the marsh. Yes, we learned, the southwestern coast of Mexico differed from the northeastern coast of the United States in something more than just the warmth of its sun and sea. There was diversity even where the jet set flourished.

But our Acapulco visit was simply another, if quite spectacular, indication that the tourist industry has become as polluting and destructive as the so-called heavy industries. The hotels, motels, hamburger joints, cocktail lounges, and gas stations steamroller the uniqueness of the community they invade, destroying the very qualities that the tourist business originally came there to exploit. Variety is smothered in the interests of efficiency. A visitor must search out the reality beneath the packaged experience as diligently as a connoisseur has to hunt up other buffs of kooky sex in a strange city. The difference is that today it is only the region's uniqueness that's become almost impossible to find.

This is true wherever a region has aggressively courted one of those industries—the temptation is to call them "carnivorous"—that tend to grow and devour the region itself. Oil, petrochemical complexes, rampant tourism all come to mind. Even the National Park Service has suffered from this sort of shortsighted development; in the rivalry among the superintendents of various parks, visitors were encouraged in such numbers that their parks' special qualities were nearly destroyed. As long ago as 1954, James P. Gilligan, a professional forester, warned against the notion that in a democracy we cannot restrict development.

"The real democratic significance of these areas," Gilligan said of the more remote and unspoiled regions of our parks, "may not be in providing access and accommodations to everyone, but in holding a few undeveloped areas where high quality recreation benefits can still be obtained by those willing to make the effort."

The same warning might have been sounded against headlong development of any kind, as we have learned since to our dismay. The enormous dislocation fragments a community or a region; and when it is finally put back together again it has lost its identity. Some people thrive in such a featureless environment. Those of us who do not must go on struggling in the hope that when change does come it does not destroy our community's natural and cultural character.

That is why we fought against the placement here of a massive oil refinery and petrochemical complex. It seemed to us to be something more than the community and the landscape could bear. Because of its size and impact, this industry would inevitably soak up the region's impulse to renew its diversity. Once there had been a great diversity of activity here—fishing, shipbuilding, logging, farming, canning, and small industries and business. As in other regions made obsolete by the modern revolution in technology, this economic diversity dwindled away, leaving us prey to all the violent fluctuations and consequent ills that are best illustrated by the "one-company town." To impose a single mammoth industry on this fragile region would be to perpetuate the absence of diversity; oil would be incompatible with the hopes for fishing, aquaculture, well-regulated tourism, and small nonpolluting industries here in the future.

Of course, Maine cannot turn its back on oil as a source of energy. Oil still comes here in large shipments by tanker and barge. Robert L. Dow, Research Director of Maine's Sea and Shore Fisheries Department, has suggested that all of the state's needs could be filled by a pipeline from other East Coast ports where terminals have already been developed. This is not a far-fetched solution. As we have seen, Portland receives from tankers and sends on to Montreal by pipeline more oil each year than is used in the entire state of Maine.

One does not have to visit Acapulco to realize that tourism unrestrained can be more pervasive in its destruction than even the oil industry. Honky-tonk towns, algae-infested lakes, and filled-in marshes bear testimony to the greed of local boosters. Maine has already moved to impose a moratorium on the building of camps around certain lakes that have begun to gag on vacationers' sewage. Shoreline zoning (probably simply a stopgap attempt until the states are able to cooperate with the federal government in a comprehensive shoreline plan) and reforms in the local property-tax system are other urgent needs. The property taxes Maine residents pay grew 9.1 per cent a year during the 1960s. Caught in this unbearable squeeze, property owners have had to sell their choice land to the developers.

"The present property tax burden, generally low incomes and declining rural industries combine to produce the kind of willy-nilly development that will destroy the very resource itself," wrote Professor Richard Barringer of the John F. Kennedy School of Government at Harvard University.* Barringer points out that Maine's local property taxes make

* Richard Barringer and others, *A Maine Manifest*, The Allagash Group, Bath, Maine, 1972.

up sixty-six per cent of the cost of education, compared to an average of fifty-five per cent in the nation. Some of Maine's poor pay ten per cent or more of their annual income in property taxes. Certainly, if the state is to educate its young adequately while preserving its land from destruction, it must assume the burden of education's cost through personal and corporate income taxes.

Meanwhile, the solutions to eastern Maine's economic troubles need not be Utopian. Science and technology, which seem to have passed this region by, may be its ultimate salvation. It is time to abandon the old-fashioned recruitment of heavy and polluting industries with promises of "water plentiful and labor docile," favored in the past by the state's Department of Economic Development. Imagination and capital are needed now to bring in electronics firms, modular-housing manufacturers, computer-software companies, printers, and other nonpolluters. An obstacle to appropriate industrial growth here in the past has been a lack of indigenous capital. (Even the state's pension funds are invested in Boston banks.) When a firm settled in Maine it was financed by outside interests, who siphoned off the profits instead of plowing them back into the local economy. Just as foreign fishermen have skimmed the cream of what Maine once thought of as its own fisheries, so outside investors have profited from Maine's other resources.

The sea remains potentially the most vital of those resources. Young men in Maine still are attracted to their fathers' professions, if given half a chance to make a living at them. Acquaculture, or fish-farming, along the state's serrated 2500-mile coastline presents unlimited opportunities to supplement the sea's natural harvest. Basing his belief on potential yields in suitable areas along the Maine coast, the biologist Robert Dow believes that under intensive management the sea would yield five hundred million dollars at the primary-producer level by 1980, and two billion dollars by 1990. Shellfish of all kinds are well suited for aquaculture (Dow even believes that certain shellfish can be cultivated in the warm-water effluent from nuclear-power plants). But oil and other polluting industries obviously will destroy this potential harvest. Since the state and federal governments subsidize the oil industry in a variety of ways, it may not be too much to ask of them to help an "environmentally neutral" industry as well.

Here, as elsewhere, the people must take a stand on what kind of community they want to live in. An obstacle to aggressive action by private citizens is the syndrome that Edward C. Banfield, Professor of Government at Harvard, has called "amoral familism": the concerns of the individual do not reach beyond the circle of his family, so that people seldom come together to work effectively for a better community. This obstacle is broadened in eastern Maine by the tendency of some of its people to feel put upon. Maine has played Ireland to Massachusetts' England. It is often hard for these "colonials" to see their own worth and their countryside's appeal. When our own community's most illustrious politician, Speaker of the House David Kennedy, was asked about the impact of a proposed oil refinery at Eastport, he replied, "What's there in Eastport to pollute?"

What he meant to say was that the city already had a pollution problem from domestic sewage and fish offal. But, in any case, he stirred up a storm in Eastport, composed partly of outraged cries and partly of expressions of agreement. But whether Kennedy was right is beside the point. Comments such as his, like those of the conservationists, have helped to spread some awareness among the local people of the depth of their problems. Better than most, these people are equipped to make social and political decisions for themselves (once they have seen that there are no simple solutions) because they have been nurtured on the town meeting as a form of local government. In too many of our towns the will to *decide* one's fate has atrophied from disuse. Even so, decisions at the annual town meetings still are often taken very seriously, aggravating tempers and creating enduring enmities.

Beyond the level of local government, the state itself is run by a "citizen legislature." The men and women who serve are not professional politicians, simply because their compensation remains a "token," and so in that sense they are amateurs. While in session, they are subject to a hard sell by the various industry lobbyists who are referred to sometimes sardonically in Augusta as "the third house." (In a recent session of the legislature, the 183 legislators were badgered and "informed" by lobbyists representing 200 different interests; the most active individual lobbyist, speaking for 14 clients, happened to be a former chairman of the Republican State Committee, while the next most active, with 13 clients, was the *current* chairman of the Republican State Committee.) Obviously, on both the community and the state level, the quality of the decisions will depend on the quality of the information supplied to the people who make them.

And what should these decisions lead to? Here, as elsewhere, it would be well to have as their object the conservation of diversity that is fast dwindling from the core of our lives. Sometimes it seems that modern freedom and affluence fill our lives with more diversity than ever before. The range of gadgets that technology has made available to us and the range of new places and acquaintances that increasing mobility brings within our reach seem nearly infinite. Yet the gadgets too often insulate us from vital experiences. As the world grows smaller the people and places grow more alike. Perhaps this is inevitable. But the real world, it seems to me, lies in good part outside the hive of human affairs, and it is there that it is most important to preserve the variousness of landscape and wildlife that act as signposts toward the roots of our being.

"I believe that conservation should mean the keeping or putting in the landscape of the greatest possible ecological variety," said Charles Elton, the great British ecologist. "In the world, in every continent or island, and so far as practical in every district. This means looking for some wise principle of co-existence between man and nature, even if it has to be a modified kind of man and a modified kind of nature." *

Man is doing his best to stamp out this diversity all over the world—there is no need here to retell all of the environmental horror stories, for every reader has been served his share. But nature is stubborn, and even resilient, if given half a chance. Here on the country's northeast margin, where, for Americans, "the place called morning lies," the struggle has started between those who would preserve the character of the natural world around them and those who would pave it over and dam it up and coat it with oil in the interest of their notion of economics.

I plead for the diversity of life and land—of tides and herons, and foxes and ferns. Years ago on a sandbar off New York's Long Island I matched up some flying birds and cracked seashells with the illustrations in a guidebook, and it was as if someone had thrown a switch, casting a bright searching beam for me into a million corners and crannies in the natural world. There are still more I hope to investigate, and many more I will never see. I know people who say that if these things are not exploited by man they are "wasted." What good, they want to know, is a tree that grows, topples, and decays, what significance has the tiger who lives out its life remote from man's prying eyes? I say that just knowing they are there enriches my own life, gives it a margin it otherwise would not have.

——

It was a pallid morning after Christmas when Ada and I led a dozen children on their winter bird count. We stood on the shore of the bay, looking for ducks and seabirds. A bitter wind swept out of the northeast, whipping tears from our eyes and heaping the ice along the shore at our feet so that we stood on the rim of an arctic sea. Great cakes of ice, square and rhomboid, created a checkerboard pattern with the smaller

* *The Ecology of Invasions by Animals and Plants*, Methuen, London, 1958.

chunks and the slushy pools they enclosed. Beyond this frozen turbulence, where the ice cakes graded into open water, a flock of black ducks drifted in stolid undulation.

"I count sixty-three," one of the little girls called over the wind.

"Sixty-four," a boy wrapped in woolen scarves called back.

Each of the children marked on his checklist a figure that squared with his own perception of the truth. We were the only human life that stirred around the bay on this blustery morning. We were ransacking its surface and the forests about it for the other life they held, naming and counting as in a game, but also reminding ourselves of the richness that persists wherever man has not put his stamp too greedily. Someone detected a loon low in the water off the rocky point, and the children clumped away over the ice cakes into the teeth of the wind. The loon would be our thirtieth species, a respectable total for our little band on such a morning.

And then the snow began. It came fitfully at first, and soon in a swirling blast that blotted out the bay. There was no longer any question of looking for birds. The tide was rising, and the waves tumbled over the heaped ice, and the wind tore at the small hooded and muffled figures around me. Yet no one retreated from the storm. Instead, the children responded with physical excitement that I had never seen in them before, their bodies light and airy in their heavy clothing as they skipped over the rocks, their voices piping cries back and forth across the storm like small birds chattering in the moment of some swift climatic change.

Snow and cold and surging tides were no novelty to these children. They had lived with them through the long winters which authors who spend but three balmy months with us specify as the bleak hand that blights our lives. But now small faces emerged from their mufflers to savor the horizontal rush of flakes. A little girl, still clutching her pencil and checklist with both hands to her belly, sprang up twice, three times, on the tips of her booted toes as if she would ride the white wind wherever it took her.

I felt scarcely earthbound myself. The storm blinded and sometimes stung. Like the others, I was wrapped in that good kind of loneliness which is a part of our confrontation with the natural world. In the lash of the storm on that exposed rocky place there were intimations of the force that still tests in each of us, when we confront it alone, our capacity to marvel at natural things and our delight in our own being. We would share this exhilarated loneliness afterward. I like to think that the magic of this storm and this special place will remain with the children in the years ahead, when they decide whether the magic will be able to renew itself again and again for other generations.